11/28

FOREWORD

When I started riding, which I am told was at a very young age, I was not old enough to worry about the safety or otherwise of what I was doing. I enjoyed the sensation of riding and the close relationship with my pony. I was lucky. Not only was I able to enjoy and appreciate ponies and subsequently horses, but my parents were knowledgeable as well and were, therefore, able to ensure that my early riding was done in comparative safety.

I say comparative safety because a horse or pony is many times more powerful, heavier and stronger than a man or child and you are inevitably, therefore, slightly at the mercy of the beast. All you can do then is to take all sensible precautions before you brave your first encounter. However, there is no guarantee that you won't be bitten, kicked or fall off but at least you can reduce the possibilities of being hurt if you do take a tumble, and the chances will then be that you will have nothing more serious than a few bruises to show off to your friends the next day!

Ann Brock in her book *Riding and Stable Safety* draws on her many and varied experiences to explain in great detail the best ways of handling horses and ponies so as to try and preserve not only your safety but that of the horse as well both while you are at home and in public places. As such it is well worth reading because the safer you feel, the more confidence you will have and that in turn will mean that you will get more enjoyment from your horse or pony. If you are able to enjoy riding and being with an animal you will build up an affection and a special relationship with it which means that it will have a very happy life.

My only regret is that this book was not written a long time ago. I would still have fallen off, still have been bitten and kicked, but perhaps if this book had been published twenty-five years ago I would have subsequently had far fewer bruises to show my friends!

I would like to wish all who read this book many happy hours of safe riding.

CAPTAIN MARK PHILLIPS

RIDING AND STABLE SAFETY

Ann Brock

David & Charles
Newton Abbot   London

Line drawings by Mrs Betty Moore
'Spot the Mistakes' illustration by Mrs Mandy Eustis
I should like to thank Bertie Hill for his kindness in suggesting
to the publishers that I be asked to write this book, and to all
those who have helped me in any way I offer my sincere thanks.

British Library Cataloguing in Publication Data

Brock, Ann
   Riding and stable safety.
   1. Horsemanship – Safety measures
   2. Horses
   I. Title
   614.8'77   SF309

ISBN 0–7153–7951–8

Typeset by Trade Linotype Limited, Birmingham
and printed in Great Britain
by Biddles Limited, Guildford
for David & Charles (Publishers) Limited
Brunel House   Newton Abbot   Devon

Contents

Introduction

A life without danger would be like St George without the dragon. Its presence is a challenge, and man's defiance of it has brought him some of his greatest achievements. If you eliminated danger, the vital spirit of mankind would wither and die.

Safety can never be guaranteed when riding a horse, and if it could, the attraction of riding would rapidly fade for most of us. There is no greater satisfaction to the true horseman or woman than winning the battle for supremacy over a really difficult horse. It is a pitting of the rider's wits, courage, patience and appreciation of the horse's mentality against the animal's superior strength. Adam Lindsay Gordon, the Australian poet, sums it up when he says :

> No game was ever worth a rap
> For a rational man to play
> Into which no accident, no mishap
> Could possibly find a way.

Would a mountaineer want to climb Everest if there was no possible risk or danger? Nevertheless, mountaineers are not foolhardy people; they take reasonable precautions to avoid accidents, and ensure their own safety as far as possible.

This book has been written to try to help newcomers to the horse world. If they are made aware of some of the dangers and pitfalls connected with riding and looking after horses, they will be able to avoid them. The lists of 'dos' and 'don'ts' on the following pages may seem daunting to the uninitiated, but in fact most of them are merely common sense, and the experienced horseman or woman would comply with them without conscious thought.

Those whose entire lives have been spent with horses will have learnt, perhaps by bitter experience, the traps that one can fall into by not taking enough trouble, or by being careless. Accidents usually happen without warning, but with a little more knowledge and care can often be avoided.

Horses are not machines that can be relied upon to obey certain rules of cause and effect, but unpredictable living creatures with their own individual idiosyncrasies, moods and feelings. The most successful horsemen and horsewomen are those who are not dogmatic and inflexible in their views, but open-minded and adaptable, and willing to concede that there are other methods than those to which they have been accustomed. Someone once said that minds are like parachutes – they only function when they are open.

There are, of course, some indisputable rights and wrongs in dealing with horses, with which no one would disagree, but there is also a vast variety of theories, beliefs and ideas which produce the same results but are very different in application. Horses are great individualists, and what suits one may not necessarily suit another. 'Going by the book' is fine, provided the horse has read the same book!

I think it would be true to say that a considerable number of accidents, especially with young horses, are caused through fear. A frightened horse is potentially a dangerous one. We should remember that in their wild state, the horses of long ago relied on their instincts of fear to alert them to danger, and when they were threatened, they either fled in panic, or defended themselves with teeth and hooves. Years of civilisation have not completely eradicated these natural instincts, and instead of condemning the horse who misbehaves as obstructive or stupid, we should look more closely at our own lack of understanding.

The difficulty in writing a book about safety is to prevent it from becoming just another dissertation on 'learning to ride' or 'horse management'. I have not delved too deeply into the details of horsemanship, which are dealt with at length in many excellent books, but mention them only in so far as they directly or indirectly affect the safety of horse or rider.

Riding has never been more popular, and encouraged by television, magazines, newspapers and the spread of riding schools and trekking establishments, more and more people are buying horses and ponies without sufficient knowledge to be able to look after them properly. It is up to those people to seek help and advice from the more experienced in order to avoid the unintentional hardship and cruelty that is all too often inflicted on the horses of today.

1

Safe Riding Wear

Having decided that you would like to learn to ride, one of your first questions is likely to be, 'What do I wear?' There is a saying that the art of being well dressed is to wear clothes that are suitable to the occasion. For riding, 'suitable' clothes must have safety as their first priority. In addition, they must be comfortable so that they do not distract the rider or in any way restrict his movements.

Fortunately, it is not necessary to buy a lot of expensive riding kit. Jeans, anoraks etc, although not ideal, are quite acceptable. Later on, of course, if you intend to ride competitively, then you will find it necessary to buy the correct clothes, but in general, if what you wear is neat, workmanlike and well-fitting, the choice is a personal one. Nevertheless, there are two items which must be considered as vital to the safety of the rider, without which he would certainly be at risk; these are a hard hat and safe footwear.

The hat

No jockey would dream of riding in a steeplechase without protective headgear, but many riders risk their lives every day by riding on dangerous roads without anything to protect their heads. Investing in a hard hat is rather like taking out an insurance; ninety-nine times out of a hundred it will not be needed, but on the hundredth occasion it could save your life.

The maxim 'experience bought is experience well taught' is very true in the riding world. Until you have fallen on your head, you may not be convinced of the importance of wearing a well-fitting cap *every time you ride*, and not just for competitive purposes. If you have a fall, you are as likely to hit your head while hacking along the road as you are in a competition.

There are many different designs of riding caps to choose from, but the important point to consider is the fit; the hat must stay in place even though you may be hanging upside down! Most of them have elastic chin straps for additional safety, but it you have to rely on the strap in order to keep the hat on, it is not the right size for you.

Here we have a slight conflict between elegance and safety. For instance, it is not 'done' to wear a chin strap for showing or dressage; in fact many adults object to wearing one at all, except for racing or cross-country work. If the cap fits correctly, an elastic should not be absolutely necessary, but there is no doubt, of course, that it is an additional safety factor. Children are always safer wearing some kind of strap under the chin – either an elastic, or the Pony Club approved safety harness, which can be attached to the cap. Understandably, parents are inclined to buy hats for children that will allow a little room for growing, in which case safety straps are absolutely vital.

The modern type of riding cap has a flexible brim which will bend if it hits the ground, preventing the whiplash effect which could possibly occur with the rigid type of brim. To fit the cap correctly, never cram it on the back of your head where it is likely to fall off, but place it well forward, with the brim horizontal to the ground.

Some riding stables keep a number of hard hats which clients can hire. This may perhaps save you the expense of buying one until you are sure you want to continue riding, but often there is not a very big selection of sizes, and you may have difficulty in finding one that will fit properly.

Keep your hair off your face, either by tying it back or by putting it into a net. Hair that is continually blowing into your eyes is not only distracting, but could obscure your vision at the critical moment.

Safe footwear

What you wear on your feet is every bit as important as what you put on your head. Never wear shoes or boots without heels,

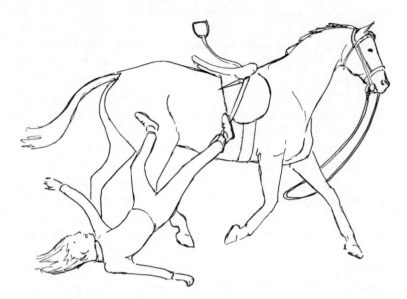

A rider being dragged because her shoe, which has no heel, has slipped right through the stirrup iron

as there is nothing to prevent the feet from slipping right through the stirrup irons. In the event of a fall, your foot could be trapped, and you would be dragged along the ground.

Sandals, plimsolls, beach shoes and shoes with wedged heels are all dangerous, as are those with buckles or fancy strappings. Any boot or shoe which cannot be slipped easily in and out of the stirrup irons is a potential trap. For this reason, boots with deeply grooved or half-soles should not be worn. Heavy Wellington boots are very dangerous as they often have thick, grooved soles. There may come a time when you will want to quit your stirrups very quickly, for example if the horse rears or slips up, and anything which prevents you from doing so is a hazard.

Also against the rules of safety, though for a different reason, are soft shoes such as slippers or moccasins, which afford no protection if you are stepped on by a horse, nor if you step on loose stones, gravel etc.

The ideal riding boot, of course, is the long leather hunting boot, which protects against bangs, kicks, and being rubbed by the leathers, but its cost today may be prohibitive, in which case a cheaper rubber version makes an excellent substitute. If you do not possess boots of any kind, ordinary strong walking shoes are quite all right, provided they have heels and smooth full soles.

The rest of your outfit

As I mentioned at the beginning of the chapter, whether you wear a hacking jacket or an anorak, breeches, jodhpurs or jeans, depends entirely on the type of riding that you intend to do and on your own preference. From the safety point of view, as long as they are comfortable, fit properly, and do not hinder you in any way, they will be acceptable.

Always ensure that there are no hanging belts, flapping accessories, or anything that may upset the horse. If you are going to ride a strange horse, make sure that he is not nervous of a long riding mac touching him behind the saddle. Some young horses will buck if they are not used to it. Another point of safety to remember is never put on a coat, or take one off, while sitting on the horse. Not only are you obliged to drop the reins, but at one stage your arms will be trapped in the sleeves, putting you in a very unsafe position.

Never wear bangles, necklaces or drooping earrings when riding or working around horses. They not only look out of place, but are liable to get caught up in something, particularly if you have a fall.

Gloves

Gloves, though by no means essential, will help to protect your hands, keep them mobile in cold weather, and give a better grip on the reins. String is ideal, but any material that is not too thick, and allows contact with the reins, with no restriction of the movement of your fingers, will be suitable. For these reasons, mittens without individual fingers are taboo.

Spurs

Novices and children should not wear spurs : in the majority of cases they have not had the experience to know how to use them. Spurs are not worn, as is generally supposed, to punish the horse, but are sometimes used by advanced riders to assist the action of the heel. For example, when schooling a horse, one of the rider's objectives is to teach him to respond to the lightest touch of the heel and lower leg. The careful use of spurs can enhance the effect of the most gentle touch, whereas the leg alone would not, possibly, evoke the same response.

Only blunt spurs are worn, and to put them on correctly the hooks should face downwards, with the long side of the spur on the outside of the boot. The straps face outwards, and the spur is worn along the seam of the boot, just below the ankle.

2

Some Basic
Safety Rules

There are some people who have a natural rapport with horses, and seem to know instinctively how to behave around them. Others, perhaps more mechanically minded, lack this affinity, and make mistakes which could put both them and the horse at risk.

It is important to remember that your safety depends on the relationship that you are able to build up with your horse. For example, an erratic, noisy or quick-tempered person can very easily upset a nervous horse, particularly a young one, whereas a quiet, confident and understanding approach will soothe his fears, and make him relaxed and receptive to your wishes.

As I said in the introduction, a lot of accidents are caused through fear on the part of either the rider or the horse. It is well known that some animals can 'smell' fear; they seem to know when a human being is frightened of them, and will react accordingly. A young horse that is being broken in, for instance, will soon sense if you are nervous of him, and will take advantage of it by playing up. On the other hand, if the horse himself is frightened, he will either panic and try to run away, or will defend himself as nature taught him, with teeth and hooves.

How to approach a horse

The manner in which you approach a horse can have a definite effect on his behaviour. Any hesitancy or apprehension on your part will make him nervous and arouse his suspicion, while a calm, direct approach will give him confidence.

A very good illustration of this is given by Colonel Podhajsky, Director of the Spanish Riding School in Vienna, in his book

My Horses, My Teachers. He tells of a particular incident which happened when he was a young man in the Austrian Cavalry School. One of the horses that he had been assigned to ride was, unknown to him, a notorious kicker, whom all the grooms approached with trepidation. One day he walked quite innocently into the mare's stall, and was happily patting her and making a fuss of her when a groom came in and reacted with horror, saying that she had laid out more than one of his colleagues who had tried to get too close. Colonel Podhajsky, unaware of her reputation, had approached her so calmly and directly that the idea of defending herself had not entered her head, whereas the grooms' attitude of fear had only aroused her suspicions.

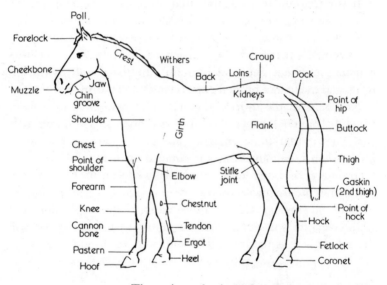

The points of a horse

It may seem obvious that you should make sure the horse knows you are there before you touch him, but accidents have been known to happen because someone has carelessly slapped a hand on a horse who was unaware of his presence. The horse may have been half asleep, or looking intently at something else. Even the most docile animal will lash out in self-defence if suddenly startled, so always speak to him quietly before you touch him.

Whenever possible approach a horse from the side, and stand at his shoulder rather than directly in front of him. The theory has been suggested that, owing to the position of his eyes at the side of his head, he is able to see you more clearly, and is therefore less nervous. It is also safer from your own point of view, as he cannot knock you over if he suddenly jumps forward.

Never pat a horse on the nose; it is one of the most sensitive parts of his anatomy, and you will either irritate or frighten him. If you want to make a fuss of him, pat him on the neck.

Be wary of any horse you do not know, and keep well clear of his hind legs. If he is tied in a stall, or in a line with other horses, where you have no alternative but to approach from behind, always remember to speak to him first, and walk firmly towards his head, being careful not to brush against his hind-quarters as you pass.

If he is out in the field, encourage him to turn towards you by offering him a piece of apple or carrot or a handful of oats, but never make a habit of giving titbits. An occasional treat will do no harm, but if indulged too much the horse will soon make a nuisance of himself by nuzzling at your pockets and pushing you around, searching for food. It is safer not to feed a horse if he is in a field with others, as it will cause jealousy and may start a kicking match.

Never give titbits to someone else's horse without permission. Holidaymakers and trippers from towns can sometimes be a menace to horse owners who keep their horses in fields next to public roads. They will insist on feeding them with totally unsuitable things such as toffees, whole apples and thick crusts of bread. Not only are these dangerous, as they can become lodged in the throat, but the horse often starts pawing at the gate, and could get his legs caught in the bars. As a safety precaution, tie some small-mesh wire securely to the bottom rungs of the gate so that he cannot get his legs through.

When carrots or apples are given to horses, they must be sliced. Carrots should be cut lengthways; round thick chunks could cause choking. If you feed a horse by hand, lay the food on the palm with the fingers lying flat and close together. If your fingers are curled around it, he may not be able to avoid biting them.

Learn to watch the expression in a horse's eyes; it can tell you a lot about his intentions and state of mind. If his eyes are placid and calm, he has every confidence in you, but if they look wild and staring and he lays back his ears, be prepared – he is either going to be aggressive, or panic is getting the upper hand. In either case, a soothing hand and quiet voice will work wonders.

Your first lesson

If you are going to a riding school to learn to ride, choose carefully. In the majority of cases, of course, the choice is limited by distance, or by the number of schools in your particular area. However, you can obtain information about the various schools from either the British Horse Society or the Association of British Riding Schools (see appendix for addresses.)

All schools have to be licensed, but some teach to a higher level than others. The British Horse Society runs a scheme for the approval of riding schools throughout the British Isles; a school can become approved, recognised or listed, and the basis on which the grading is granted is as follows:

Approved
The establishment (which is licensed by the local authority) offers sound instruction in riding and horsemastership at whatever level on well-cared-for horses and ponies, which are the property of the school, and the premises are clean and properly run. Any riding school which has been operating for twelve months and fulfils the above requirements is eligible for inclusion on the approved list.

Recognised
The horses and ponies are well cared for, and the premises are properly run. It can also be recognised for some particular or specialised facility or service it offers to members of the

riding public. All riding establishments, livery yards, training or facility centres, riding holidays establishments and trekking centres which have been operating for twelve months and fulfil the above requirements are eligible for inclusion on the recognised list.

Listed

Must hold a valid licence, issued by the local licensing authority.

So you can see that if you want to learn to ride properly, as opposed to just going out for a hack, it would be advisable to find a school which is approved.

You can quite easily judge for yourself whether a school is of a high standard or not. Note carefully the condition of the horses and ponies, and how the tack is cared for. Rough and ready schools that allow their clients to ride out on the roads unescorted, with no hard hats, and wearing gym shoes, are unlikely to be very particular in any other respect, and your safety is obviously not their first concern.

The impression one gets when walking into any stable yard should be one of neatness and efficiency, with the horses not only physically in good condition, but also completely relaxed. I once paid a visit to a stable and the first thing I saw was a horse tied to a tree with a thin piece of binder twine looped around his neck. After picking my way amongst the stable forks, buckets, dogs' feeding bowls and various bits of debris lying on the ground, I eventually found the horse that I had come to see, standing gloomily in the middle of his box with a chicken on his back! The owner then leapt on him bareback, and proceeded to gallop down a hard road to show me how he could move. Needless to say, his legs were already beginning to show signs of the treatment he had been receiving. This establishment, I may hastily add, was obviously not a riding school, but a private yard. The conditions in which the horses lived there were a disgrace to anyone calling himself a horseman.

It is very important to let the instructor know that you have had no previous experience. Even if you have been on a horse a

few times before, never pretend that you can ride. If you over-
estimate your ability, you may be assigned a horse which is not
suitable for a novice, and the inevitable accident will occur.
Most riding schools are very careful about suiting horse to rider,
and if you are honest, your safety will be their primary concern.

Tying a horse safely

Before you actually mount, there are many things to be learnt
about the general handling of horses. Mistakes can put both
horse and pupil at risk.

For example, one of your first lessons should be on how to
tie up a horse with the correct knot, which is one that can be
quickly released in an emergency. Some horses, especially young
ones, have an innate fear of being tied. As I explained in the
introduction, although horses have been tamed and civilised for
many years, they still retain many of the instincts of their
ancestors. A tied horse feels trapped, and if he is frightened he
may try to pull away. It has been known for a young horse to
panic and fight so hard that he has actually broken his neck by
throwing himself over. For this reason it is safer to tie the lead
rope to a loop of binder twine (C in the diagram) than directly
to the ring in the loose box or the fence in the field. The twine
will be strong enough to hold the horse in place, but will break
under extreme pressure. It is better to have a loose horse than a
dead one! Of course, this precaution is more important with
young horses; the majority of older ones will stand tied quite
happily.

The quick-release knot (A and B in the diagram) should be
learnt so thoroughly that it becomes automatic every time you
tie up a horse. It may be easier to learn to tie it if some more
experienced person can demonstrate it to you. As you can see,
the knot is perfectly secure, but can be released by a jerk of the
spare end. A word of warning though! If you are able to release
the horse easily, he too will be able to set himself free by tugging
at the spare end with his teeth. In order to counteract this, slip
the loose end through the loop (D in the diagram), so that even

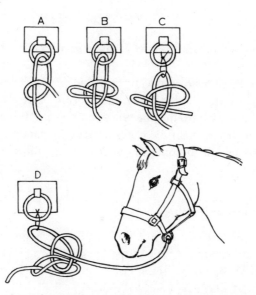

The correct release knot. (A and B) how to tie the knot; (C) the rope tied to a loop of binder twine for greater safety, particularly with young horses; (D) the end of the rope slipped through the loop so that the horse cannot free himself

if the horse plays with it, it will not come loose. This knot should also be used when tying up a haynet.

You may be wondering why, if the knot is so effective as a quick-release device, it should ever be necessary to tie a horse to something that will break in an emergency (ie the loop of binder twine). The reason is this. If a horse panics suddenly, he will pull back on the rope with all his weight, causing the knot to become so tight that it will be difficult to undo in a hurry.

Never tie a horse with such a long rope that he is able to get a leg over it or to turn round. At the same time, he must have enough room to move his head freely. He should, of course, never be tied to anything that will move or roll around and frighten him. Tying a horse to the ramps of a lorry, or the door of any vehicle, for instance, is a dangerous practice.

Always ensure that he is tied by the rope of a headcollar or halter, and never by the reins of the bridle. If he pulled back, he would not only smash the bridle, but could also injure his mouth. If he already has a bridle on, slip a headcollar over it, and tuck the reins behind the stirrup leathers so that he cannot step on them.

Never leave a horse tied up for long periods on his own, and check to see that he is not exposed to cold, draughts or hot sun. If there are flies around, he will soon become frustrated if he is unable to reach them. Also ensure that he cannot be kicked by other horses, or become entangled in anything lying on the ground.

Headcollars and halters

A headcollar is usually made of leather or nylon, and the lead rope is attached to a ring at the back of the noseband. A halter is made of rope or webbing, and the lead rope is a continuation of the part that goes round the nose.

If you are using a halter, it is important to remember to tie a knot at the point shown in the diagram on p. 23. This prevents the rope from tightening round the nose and causing pain, or even severe injury, in the event of a horse pulling back.

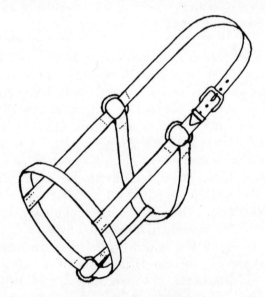

The leather headcollar

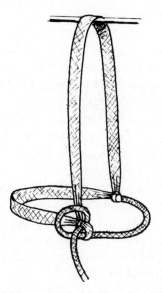

The webbing halter, showing the safety knot

Make sure that the headcollar or halter fits correctly. If it is too large, it can easily be pulled off, and the part which goes round the nose will be too low, and will irritate the sensitive membranes above the nostrils. Also, in the case of the halter, the rope will rub the horse's eyes. If too small, it will rub the cheekbones and constrict the horse's jaw.

Putting on the saddle

There is a right way and a wrong way to do almost everything connected with horses. The wrong way threatens your safety; the right way helps to ensure it. It is important that you get into the habit of doing things correctly, so that this becomes automatic. Older, experienced horses are usually long-suffering, and will put up with your mistakes, but a young one may turn a careless error into a fatal one.

Putting on the saddle correctly is an excellent example. If not enough care is taken, a young horse may start bucking and the rider could be thrown. Some horses, even older ones, suffer from a condition known as 'cold back': unless the saddle is given time to warm to the horse's back before he is ridden, he will tense up, and will often rear or buck. For this reason the saddle is put on before the bridle; the horse should be tied up with a headcollar to prevent him from moving around.

Before you saddle up, ensure that the girth is placed neatly over the seat and that the stirrups are 'run up'. To run up the stirrup irons, take hold of the lower part of the stirrup leather and slide the iron up underneath as far as it will go. Then push the whole of the leather, including the spare end, down through the iron; this will hold the iron in place.

Running up the irons is a very important safety measure, and should be done every time you dismount. Dangling irons are dangerous, for the following reasons. They might frighten the horse by banging against his sides; they could get caught up on any protruding object such as a gate latch or door handle; they could knock against the sides of the doorway as you lead the horse through, and startle him; and lastly, but certainly not least important, a horse could easily get either his bit or his teeth caught in a stirrup iron if he turned round to bite at something. I have actually seen this happen: the horse in

'Run up' stirrups

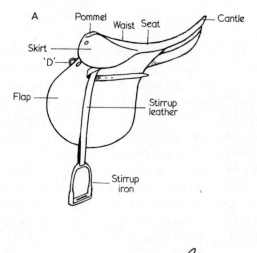

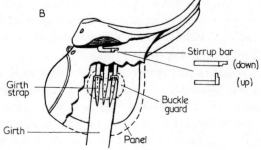

The parts of the saddle (A), including a cutaway view (B)

question reached round to bite at some flies, and somehow managed to hook his bit on to the iron. He immediately panicked, and started to rush round in a circle trying to free himself. Luckily, he did so before he was injured.

It does not really matter from which side the horse is saddled, but in order to save time it is more convenient to stand on the off (right) side of the horse. As the girth should already be attached to that side of the saddle, you can check to see that it is lying flat, and that everything is straight and not rucked up underneath the saddle flap, before going round (in front of the horse, not behind) to the near (left) side to fasten the girth.

Make sure the horse's back is clean and free from dried mud, sweat or grit, particularly if you have just brought him in from the field. A sore back is an understandable excuse for a horse to buck. Stand close to his shoulder, and place the saddle well forward near the withers, so that as you slide it back into the correct position, the hair will be left lying flat and comfortable. The correct position is more or less in the deepest part of the back, leaving the shoulders free of any interference, and the loins free of any pressure from the saddle.

Let the girth down carefully, avoiding any knocks against the forelegs; then return to the near side and fasten it to the girth straps. Do not girth too tightly at first, as this will encourage the horse to 'blow himself out', expanding his body against the girth. Do it up just tightly enough to prevent the saddle from slipping back or sideways. You will have to tighten it again before you mount. See that it is not pinching or rucking up the horse's skin by running your fingers down inside it. Another way of ensuring that the skin is not wrinkled is to pick up each foreleg in turn and gently pull it forward; this will stretch the skin and eliminate any wrinkles.

The fitting of a saddle is of the utmost importance. If the horse is uncomfortable or in pain, he will be liable to show his resentment by trying to get rid of the rider! Ensure that the pommel (front arch) is high enough to clear the withers and is not pinching or putting any pressure on them, particularly when the weight of the rider is pressing on the saddle. There must be no pressure on the horse's spine or on the loin area. The saddle must be supported by the muscles on either side, which cover the upper part of the ribs. To check this, stand in front and slightly to one side of the horse, and look back through the pommel to the underpart of the saddle. There should be a clear space above the spine, so that you can see daylight right through to the back.

Some saddles are worn too far forward, interfering with the free movement of the shoulders. If you are in doubt as to whether the saddle fits, ask an experienced person to check it for you.

Always remember to place the saddle gently on the horse's back; by banging it down roughly, you will either frighten him or make his back sore.

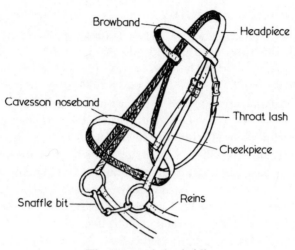

The parts of the bridle

Putting on the bridle

The importance of taking time and trouble to put on a bridle carefully cannot be over-stressed. Many horses become permanently head-shy as a result of rough treatment. It is really a very simple operation if done correctly, but I have seen people getting into all kinds of trouble with horses who throw up their heads, won't open their mouths, and back away from the bridle.

I think one of the main reasons for this is that the riders have not been taught to put the bridle on in the correct way – that is, the way which gives the most control over the horse's head. Many books on horses, I am sorry to say, advocate a method which, to my mind, is completely impractical, and is very often the cause of difficulties. I will outline this method briefly after explaining the safe procedure.

The most practical and logical method of putting on a bridle is as follows. First, see that the noseband is unfastened; this allows more freedom to manipulate the bridle. Place the reins over the horse's neck; if you put them halfway up the neck, you will have more control if he tries to pull away. Stand on the near side, just behind his head and facing towards the front. Holding the bridle in your left hand, pass your right hand *round*

the back of the horse's jaw, to reach round to the front of his
nose. In this way, if he tries to raise his head or swing it from
side to side, your right hand is on his nose to prevent it. Now,
transfer the bridle to your right hand, holding it by the cheekpieces halfway up the bridle, and with your left hand, gently
insert the bit in the horse's mouth. If he refuses to open it, press
your left thumb lightly into the corner of his mouth where there
are no teeth; this will make him open his mouth without any
trouble. Take your time and don't bang the bit roughly against
his teeth, but guide it carefully between them. Then, with both
hands, ease the headpiece over his ears, ensuring that the mane
is sorted out and lying flat and comfortable.

Do up the throat lash, not too tightly, as it will interfere with
the horse's breathing; if you can put your wrist between it and

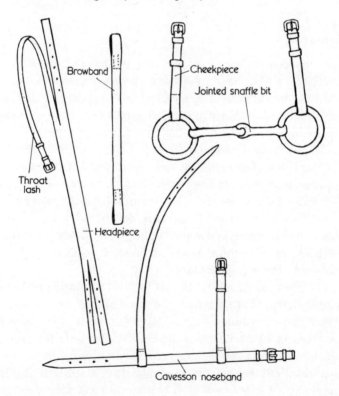

The bridle dismantled to show its construction

The correct way to put on a bridle, ensuring adequate control of the horse's head

the throat, it will be correct. Its function is to prevent the bridle from slipping over the horse's head.

Finally, fasten the noseband so that you are able to insert two fingers between the noseband and the front of the nose; if it is too tight the horse will be unable to move his jaw. Make sure that it is not so high that it rubs the projecting cheekbones; about 2in (5cm) below them is correct. There are several different types of noseband, each having a specific purpose, but the most commonly used is the plain cavesson, to which, if needed, a martingale can be attached (see chapter 8).

The bit must be the correct height in the mouth – high enough to touch the corners of the mouth but not wrinkle the skin. If it is too low, it will bang against the incisor (front) teeth.

The other method of putting on the bridle, mentioned earlier, affords no control over the horse's head if he tries to move it away from you or lifts it up higher than you can reach. This entails holding the headpiece of the bridle in the *right* hand, and *in front of* the horse's head, and then inserting the bit in the manner already described. By not having one hand free to hold his nose at the beginning of the procedure, you immediately lose all control of his head. I am surprised that this method is even mentioned in official Pony Club books, as it makes it very difficult for any child to bridle a pony successfully.

The correct methods of saddling and bridling have been described in some detail because, if these things are done haphazardly, they can cause the horse acute discomfort, putting the safety of the rider at risk.

Leading the horse correctly

Lack of care when leading a horse, especially if he is excited, can result in an accident. Remember, a stabled horse is often eager to get out, and may try to rush through the door. Always take the reins forward over his head first – lifting them, not dragging them, over his ears – so that you have more length of rein with which to hold him if he tries to play up. Make sure that he comes squarely through the door, and not at an angle where he may hit his hip bone or get his saddle caught in the door jamb. The stirrups, of course, must still be in the run-up position so that there is no possibility of them banging against his sides or becoming caught in the door.

For maximum control hold the reins about 6in (15cm) below the bit, but if your horse has been well-schooled you can allow him a little more freedom for his head. Never lead a horse by holding on to any part of the bridle or headcollar itself, but only by the reins or lead rope. If your fingers were curled around the bit, for example, and the horse suddenly jerked his head up, he would wrench himself free, and probably injure your fingers at the same time. Never twist the reins, or the lead rope if using a headcollar, round your hands; if the horse bolted, you would have difficulty in getting free. If leading with a rope, a simple knot at the end would give you a better grip in an emergency.

Do not walk directly in front of the horse, in case he jumps forward, but a little to one side. If he is reluctant to move, do not get in front of him and pull – he will always be the winner in a tug-of-war – but instead, encourage him to go forward by using your stick, which should be carried in your left hand (assuming that you are leading from the near side). Bring it behind your back and tap him with it behind the girth. In order to leave your hand free to use the stick, you will have to transfer

Leading a horse correctly

the spare end of the reins to your right hand.

Horses are usually led from the near side, for which the above instructions are correct. If, however, you lead one on a public highway, he must be led from the off side, and the reins and stick, of course, will be held in the opposite hands.

Sometimes it may be necessary to lead a horse up and down for a vet to inspect for lameness, or perhaps later on you may wish to show one, in which case you will be required to run him out for the judge to assess his movement. Lack of experience is often shown up by the manner in which someone leads his horse at a show. In both instances, lead him from the near side in the way that has been described, making sure that there is no surplus rein trailing on the ground where the horse could step on it or you could become entangled.

Always look ahead and watch where you are going. If running the horse out in front of a vet or judge, keep him in a straight line. When turning, slow up, then push his head *away* from you, ie to the right; in this way he will remain balanced and under control as you turn him round, whereas if you drag his head towards you, he will swing his quarters out and is much more likely to get out of control. (This mistake often identifies an 'unhorsey' person in the show ring.) When trotting him back, go *directly* towards the judge or vet so that he can assess the horse's movement from the front. Many competitors in the show ring, particularly children, make it difficult for the judge to see the horse from the front, as they tend to wander off course instead of coming straight back to him.

The safe way to mount

Before you mount any horse, make it a golden rule to *check the girth*. This is quite easy to remember if you learn to associate run-up stirrups with loosened girths; the two should always go together. When the horse is first brought out of the stable the stirrups should be up, and the girth not yet tight enough; when you return from your ride and dismount, your first task must be to run up your stirrups and loosen the girth. This will soon become second nature.

You are probably wondering how tight the girth should be. It must be tight enough to prevent the saddle from slipping round as you put your weight on the stirrup, but not too tight for the horse's comfort. If you are just able to slip two fingers between it and the horse's body, it will be correct. Remember that when your weight comes on to the saddle, it will probably need to come up another hole.

When tightening the girth, don't forget to loop the reins over your arm so that you still have the horse under control.

Before you mount check the stirrup bar (see B in the figure on p. 25) to ensure that the hinge is straight and not turned up. If it is up, the stirrup leather is prevented from slipping off in an emergency, and in the event of a fall you would be in danger of being dragged should your foot become caught in the iron.

Make sure that the stirrups are the correct size for your feet. They should be large enough to allow the feet to slip easily in and out, but not so large that they could slip right through. About $\frac{1}{2}$in (1cm) clearance on each side of the foot is right.

Initially everyone is taught to mount from the near side. This stems from the days when knights and cavalrymen wore their swords on the left hip; if they had tried to mount from the off side, the sword would have got in the way as they swung their leg over. It would add to your dexterity if you learnt to mount from both sides, and you never know when it may come in useful; but do not experiment on an unfamiliar horse, as he may not appreciate your endeavours.

To mount correctly, stand beside the horse's near shoulder, facing the tail. In this position he cannot kick you. Pick up the reins in the left hand, holding them just taut enough to prevent the horse from moving forward. If you are carrying a stick, hold this too in your left hand, allowing it to hang down by the horse's left shoulder. Throw the excess rein over to the other side of the neck to ensure that you do not become entangled in it. Place the left hand on the withers, and with the right hand take the part of the stirrup which is nearest the horse's tail and turn it towards you. Put your left foot in the stirrup, being careful not to dig your toe into the horse's side, and transfer your right hand as far over to the other side of the seat of the saddle as you can reach. Hop once on to your right foot before springing lightly into the saddle. If you try to make it in one jump, you will find that you have to hang on to the cantle of the saddle and will be inclined to pull it sideways. By hopping once you can reach further round the seat and the saddle will not become twisted.

Be careful as you swing the right leg over that you do not touch the horse's croup, as this might upset a nervous animal. As you swing your leg over, transfer your right hand to the skirt of the saddle on the off side, and sit down gently in the lowest part of the saddle. Place your right foot in the stirrup, ensuring that the leather is not twisted (a common mistake that beginners often make). Now sort out your reins, checking that they too are not twisted, but lie flat against the horse's neck.

Before you move off, always check the girth again, as your weight in the saddle will slightly loosen it. To tighten it from either side, lift one foot, still in the stirrup, forward in front of the saddle flap. Holding reins and stick in the opposite hand, lift up the flap and pull up the girth. Do not girth too tightly : there should be enough room to slide two fingers between the girth and the horse's body. Make sure the girth buckles are about the same height on each side and are resting on the panel of the saddle. If the girth is too short for the size of horse, the buckles will not reach the panel and will pinch the horse's sides. The buckle guard must be pulled down on each side; this prevents the buckle from rubbing a hole in the saddle flap.

Ensure that your stirrup leathers are the correct length. As a rough guide, stretch your legs down straight : the tread (base) of the irons should reach to just below your ankle bones. Try to get into the habit of riding with *as long a leg as is comfortable.* If the leathers are too long, you will be thrown forward; if too short, your weight will be pushed to the back of the saddle, and your legs cannot be used effectively. You will soon find the length that makes you feel most secure, but remember that the longer the leg, the easier it will be to give the correct aids (signals) to the horse.

To shorten a stirrup leather, keep your foot in the iron, but without pressing down on it. Holding the reins and stick in one hand, pull up your leather to the required length, and make sure the buckle is up against the stirrup bar. To lengthen, release the tongue from the buckle, press down hard with your foot against the iron, and allow the leather to slide down to the required length.

Dismounting safely

You may think that no risk could possibly be attached to getting off a horse, but in fact, if it is not done correctly, there are several ways in which an accident could occur.

To dismount safely, first of all ensure that your horse is standing still; never attempt to get off while he is moving. Then, *take both feet out of the stirrups.* This is a vitally important safety measure which guarantees that you cannot be hung up by the stirrup if the horse is suddenly startled. Now, with your reins and stick in your left hand, place the hand on the horse's neck just in front of the withers, while at the same time putting your right hand on the pommel of the saddle; leaning forward, vault lightly off, taking care not to kick the horse as you bring your right leg over his croup. Keep a hold on the reins throughout, and don't forget to run up your stirrups immediately and loosen the girth.

No other method of dismounting is to be recommended. One sometimes sees a rider take the right foot only out of the stirrup and step down, leaving the left foot still in the iron until the right foot touches the ground. The danger of this method is obvious : if the horse is suddenly frightened, and jumps forward, the left foot could be trapped and the rider dragged. The second method, which is seen quite often, is to drop the reins entirely and throw the right leg over the horse's neck. The danger of this is also apparent : if the horse flings his head up or moves at the wrong moment, the rider will be caught off balance and might fall; having dropped the reins, he has completely lost control of the horse.

The techniques of riding

It is not the purpose of this book to teach all the technicalities of riding – the way to hold the reins, the different aids to make the horse perform various movements, and so on – but of course mistakes in these areas, as in others, can endanger the rider's safety. Obviously, your best guarantee of safety is to learn to ride as well as possible. A good rider is less likely to make the kind of mistake that will put him at risk.

For instance, your position in the saddle is of great importance. If your seat (position) is not firm, supple and balanced, you will be forced to depend on the reins for support. Not only will this injure the horse's mouth, but you will never be able to develop the light, sensitive touch on the reins, known as 'good hands', which is the very essence of good riding. Hands, of course, are of no use on their own; they must be used in conjunction with the seat, back and legs.

Your aim should be to stay in balance and harmony with the horse through all his paces and activities. In order to achieve this, sit well down in the central and lowest part of the saddle, with your body upright but free from any stiffness. Keep your head up, with eyes looking always in the direction in which you want to go.

Keep the knees and thighs close to the saddle, but with no

exaggerated pressure. Grip can be applied instantly in an emergency, but the good rider uses balance, suppleness, poise and a sense of rhythm in preference to a vice-like grip, which tends to make the whole body stiff. The lower leg should hang naturally, but avoid a tendency to let it slide forward. If the stirrup leathers are vertical, the legs are in the correct position to be used when necessary, just behind the girth. Hold the stirrup iron on the ball of the foot, with the heel below the level of the toes, allowing maximum flexibility of the ankles. The toes should not point outwards, as this brings the knee away from the saddle; try to point them to the front as much as possible.

The arms too should hang naturally, with the forearms forming a straight line through the reins to the horse's mouth. The hands, with thumbs uppermost, are held just above the pommel of the saddle, with wrists and fingers supple, ready to follow the movements of the horse's head.

The teaching of riding, like that of many other subjects, has changed considerably over the years. As its techniques have been studied more closely, some of the old-fashioned ideas have been discarded in favour of more progressive ones. As an example, not long ago the pupil was told that grip was one of the primary requirements of riding, and was even given objects such as pennies to place between knee and saddle : woe betide anyone who lost the penny because he was not gripping tightly enough! Nowadays, the emphasis is on balance and suppleness, and grip, though of course necessary to a certain extent, is only essential in an emergency, for example if the horse shies or bucks. The theory is that through concentrating primarily on grip, the rider's whole body – particularly the legs – becomes rigid and stiff. The attitude of the rider has a direct influence on the horse, a fact which you will be able to appreciate more fully when you eventually start schooling young horses.

I have listened to many instructors teaching beginners to ride, and have found that they often tell the pupil what to do, but fail to explain why. For example, they will say 'Keep your toes up', but seldom give the reason why it is better to keep them up than down. The following are some of the mistakes most commonly made by the beginner, together with the reasons why they should be corrected. Most of them affect the security of the rider's seat, and thus his control over his horse, which in turn affects his own safety.

Pointing the toes down

If the toes are allowed to drop down, the muscles on the inside of the thighs relax. As you bring them up, the muscles tighten, giving a firmer natural grip.

Lower leg sliding forward

When the leg is forward, it is ineffective. To be of use it must be close to the horse's sides, so that it can be used instantly, without apparent movement.

Hard hands

A rider is said to have 'hard hands' if he is continually pulling or jerking the reins. If the bit is constantly bruising the 'bars' (soft gum between the incisor and molar teeth) of the mouth, the sensitive nerves in this area will eventually be destroyed and the horse will lose all feeling, thus getting a 'hard mouth'. He will then be difficult to stop.

General attitude of stiffness

The hallmark of a good rider is looking relaxed, supple and completely at ease. If your body, hands and legs are stiff, you will be unable to 'go with your horse' and follow his movement in a supple 'give-and-take' manner.

Looking down instead of ahead

If you look down, your shoulders tend to become hunched, and your seat bones cannot be pressed firmly into the saddle; you therefore lose your driving aid.

Falling to one side

This fault is seen more often than any other. Instead of sitting squarely, the rider allows one shoulder to drop, thus putting

more weight on that side. For example, if cantering in a circle
to the right, the tendency of many riders is to lean towards the
right, with their heads bent to that side. This has the effect of
upsetting the horse's balance and making him drift into the
centre of the circle.

Leaning forward to increase pace

The importance of using the back and seat bones in riding
cannot be stressed too strongly. It is with them, in conjunction
with the legs, that the rider controls the 'back end' of the horse.
In order to increase the pace, and at the same time keep the
horse balanced, the rider must push the horse's hind legs more
deeply underneath him so that they can take more of his weight.
(The untrained horse carries most of his weight on his forehand.) If the rider is leaning forward, his seat bones are brought
off the saddle and he is no longer able to use them as a driving
force.

Leaning forward at the canter

All the above remarks apply to the rider's position at the canter
with regard to the effect it has on the horse. It also has a decided
effect on his own comfort. Try this experiment for yourself.
When cantering, lean forward: you will find yourself bumping
up and down. Now, sit down firmly in the saddle, and bring
your shoulders back so that you are sitting upright. If your back
is supple, and gives to the motion of the horse, you will find that
you are in complete rhythm and harmony with his movements.

Rising too far out of the saddle in trot

There are two ways of riding at the trot: 'sitting', when the
rider's seat stays in the saddle, and 'rising', sometimes known as
'posting', when the rider rises in the stirrups as one diagonal
pair of the horse's legs comes to the ground. (When the horse
trots, he moves his legs in diagonal pairs, the near-fore and off-
hind legs moving together, and vice versa. These are known as
'diagonals', the right diagonal being the off-fore and near-hind
legs, and the left diagonal the near-fore and off-hind.)

The rider can choose to bring his seat down into the saddle either when the off-fore comes to the ground (riding on the right diagonal) or when the near-fore comes to the ground (riding on the left diagonal). In fact, the good rider should frequently change diagonals in order to rest the horse's back. This may sound very complicated; in the early stages, you will not be conscious of what the horse's legs are doing, but with the help of the instructor you will soon get the idea of rising up and down in rhythm with the movement of the trot, and will find it an easy motion. The mistake which the majority of learners make is to rise too high above the saddle, thus losing contact with the horse unnecessarily. They, in fact, try too hard. Allow the horse to do most of the work by throwing your body up himself. Some horses are more difficult to sit close to than others.

There are various ways in which you can help yourself to develop a strong, independent seat. One excellent way is to get an assistant who is very experienced to 'lunge' your horse (see chapter 15) while you ride him without reins or stirrups.

There are also a number of exercises which have been devised to improve suppleness, balance and grip. Be very careful, however, to practise for short periods only at first, otherwise you will risk strained muscles. It is also important to ensure that your horse is quiet and reliable. If you start flinging your arms around on him he may misunderstand your 'aids' and perform the 'bolt' instead of the 'halt'!

To supple body and develop thigh muscles
1   With both arms outstretched and raised to shoulder level, swing round as far as possible from the waist, at the same time bringing the head round as far as it will go. Do this to both right and left, ensuring that the knees and legs remain still, with the feet in the stirrups and the leathers hanging straight down.
2   Bend forward from the hips as low as possible, so that your head goes down beside the horse's neck, on both left and right sides. (Try to touch the horse's knee with your hand.)

3 Raise your right arm above your head, then swing forward and downward to touch the right toe. Repeat with the left arm. It is essential that your legs remain still; if they are allowed to move backwards, the whole object of the exercise is lost.

4 Repeat this exercise, but touch the opposite toe.

To loosen knee and ankle joints

5 Remove each foot from the stirrup in turn, and swing the lower leg back, bringing the heel upwards to the level of the horse's back. The knee must remain firmly on the saddle.

6 Remove each foot from the stirrup in turn and rotate both clockwise and anticlockwise. Repeat with both feet simultaneously.

To improve balance

7 Remove both feet from stirrups and lift both legs simultaneously away from the horse's sides as far as possible, so that you are balancing entirely on your seat bones. Do this first at the halt, then at the walk; it is not advisable to try at a faster pace until you have had considerably more experience. It is important that you do not rely on the reins for support; if you find that you are losing your balance, hold on to the front of the saddle.

8 Stand up in the stirrups with your legs hanging straight down; the knees must grip firmly. Try not to lean forward, but again, do not use the reins for support. This exercise can be performed with arms crossed, outstretched, etc, and at the walk, trot or canter, but do not be too ambitious at first. Avoid accidents by gradually building up your muscles and improving your balance.

Unless your horse is 'bombproof' and unlikely to put his head down to eat at the crucial moment, it would be in the interests of safety to have an assistant to either hold him still or lead him round while these exercises are being performed.

3

Safety on
the Roads

There is no such thing as 'safety on the roads'! In this modern
age, major roads have become so dangerous, with lorries, speed-
ing cars, motor bikes and so on, that your only guarantee of
safety is to keep away from them. However, even minor roads
and lanes have their share of traffic, and you never know when
you may meet a tractor, milk lorry or some farm implement, so
make sure, before you ride on any road used by the public, that
your standard of riding will enable you to control your horse in
any normal situation. You should have a firm seat, independent
of either reins or stirrups, so that if your horse shies suddenly and
you lose your irons, you will not fall off.

You must also be confident enough to ride with one hand on
the reins when necessary, leaving the other free to give your
signals to other road users. Never ride a horse on the road if you
are apprehensive – your nervousness will communicate itself to
the animal and he will inevitably take advantage of it.

It is dangerous to ride any horse on the road if he is over-
fresh, even if you are an exceptionally competent rider. A horse
who would normally ignore the most frightening lorry will play
up if he is over-fed and under-exercised. If he has just come out
of the stable, give him time to settle down first, either by
lungeing or by riding him somewhere away from traffic.
Remember that many vehicle drivers have no idea that horses
are likely to shy, so it is your responsibility to take every possible
precaution to ensure your own safety.

Before your ride

Before you go out, check the following:
1 That your tack is correctly fitted, comfortable and in good
   repair.

2   That the horse's shoes are not too worn or loose.
3   That you are wearing a hard, well-fitting hat, and full-soled
    boots or shoes with heels.
4   That you are fully covered by insurance. This is an important
    point, as you could, in certain circumstances, be held respon-
    sible for any damage that your horse might do to person or
    property.
5   That you have studied the Highway Code, and know the
    meanings of the different road signs. Although riding a
    horse, you must still obey traffic lights, pedestrian-controlled
    lights, give way signs etc.

Ride on the left

There used to be some controversy as to which was the safer side
of the road on which to ride a horse, but it seems to me that
the most recent edition of the Highway Code has the logical
answer. If you ride on the left, the oncoming traffic is not
directly in front of the horse, but slightly on one side, giving the
rider at least a small measure of leeway in which to manoeuvre.
Also, if the horse is frightened by the vehicle behind him, he will
be inclined to increase his speed *away* from it, giving the driver
a few seconds in which to brake. If the rider were on the righthand side, the horse would be more likely to whip round in
front of the vehicle and the rider could be thrown directly into
its path. To add to the hazard, horse and vehicle would be
moving *towards* one another, and those few extra seconds of
braking time would be lost.

Stay alert

Stay alert and ride your horse to the best of your ability. Never
let him slop along on a loose rein; if something suddenly frightened him he would be out of control. Keep both hands on the
reins (unless signalling), and try to prevent him from swinging
his quarters out into the traffic.
    Always be prepared for the unexpected, such as a dog running

out from a gateway or a bird flying suddenly out of a hedge. Plastic bags are a particular menace, especially in windy weather, when they always seem to flap just as your horse gets near them. Being prepared does not imply that you should ride as though there is a hazard around every corner. The more relaxed you are, the more relaxed your horse will be. A good rider can be perfectly at ease, yet at the same time be ready for any emergency.

If you see something ahead at which you think your horse might shy, don't tense up and let him assume that you are expecting trouble; you may well provoke it. Just sit normally and ride him past quietly. If he shies, ride him up to the object and allow him to inspect it : by shouting or hitting him, you will only increase his fears and confirm his suspicions. Always make sure that there is no traffic approaching or coming from behind before riding past an object that you suspect will scare your mount.

Never fight a horse on a busy road : you will be a danger both to yourself and to other road users. If he refuses to go past something, wait until the road is clear, and then be firm and determined. Sit well down in the saddle – do not lean forward – and drive him on with your legs. If the road is not slippery, and there is a lull in the traffic, then make sure that you are the victor. To give in to him would undermine your discipline and store up future trouble. If, however, the traffic is continuous, then for safety's sake dismount and lead him past, placing yourself between the horse and the traffic, and at the same time giving the motorists the slowing-down signal.

If you see that a driver is coming too fast, especially in the case of a lorry or motor bike, slow him down well in advance. If you leave it too late, he will have to brake suddenly and will probably frighten your horse. Lorries with air brakes are particularly alarming.

Always signify your intentions clearly by giving the correct signals. Do not take it for granted that the motorist has observed the signals that you have given – it is possible that he may ignore them. Be safe – always look over your shoulder to ensure that

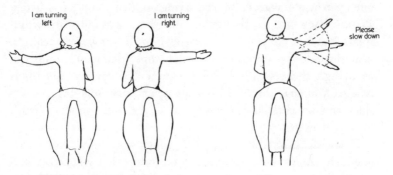

The correct hand signals for use when riding on the road

the traffic is going to slow down before you stop or move out into the road.

If you have to cross a busy road, wait quietly until it is clear. Make sure that you have time to walk across. Never try to beat the traffic by trotting; your horse will soon learn to anticipate, and it may become a bad habit.

Be careful when approaching cross-roads. If you wish to turn right, do not drift into the middle of the road as you would if driving a car, but keep close to the left-hand side until you are beyond the centre of the junction, and then turn directly across, so that you can proceed in a straight line along the left-hand side of the road to your right. Ensure that the road is clear in all directions, and give your signals in good time.

When negotiating a roundabout, keep to the left lane, and give way to all traffic on your right. When passing a stationary vehicle, look behind and in front, and give it plenty of room; the driver may suddenly open his door.

Be considerate to all pedestrians, especially children. Never ride too close, or allow them to get too close to your horse. Remember that they have the right of way on a pedestrian crossing.

Do not ride on pavements or ornamental grass verges. When riding on ordinary verges at the side of the road, be careful of narrow ditches. If allowed to become overgrown they are difficult to see, and may cause a horse to fall. Do not let your horse snatch at grass, overhanging branches, or roadside hedges; not only is it an annoying habit, but they may have been sprayed with chemicals that could be poisonous.

Never canter on the road; the horse may get excited, and the tarmac will jar his legs. Trotting downhill on a hard road is not advisable, especially if the road is slippery, but trotting uphill is an excellent muscling exercise.

SAY THANK YOU TO DRIVERS WHO SLOW DOWN FOR YOU, AND BE COURTEOUS AT ALL TIMES. This is far more important than you may realise. If you ignore a considerate driver, he may become so annoyed that he refuses to slow down for the next rider he meets, and your bad manners could be the cause of an accident. A SMILE AND A 'THANK YOU' COULD SAVE SOMEONE'S LIFE.

Riding in groups

When you ride with others you have an extra responsibility; their safety as well as yours depends on how you behave. Never do anything to upset the other horses in the group or 'ride'. If you hit or shout at your horse, you may frighten the others.

Ride in single file on narrow or busy roads, and ensure that there is a safe distance (at least a horse's length) between you and the horse in front. If you get kicked it will be your own fault.

Never let your attention be diverted by becoming too engrossed in conversation – it is often when you are off guard that the unexpected happens.

Place the quietest horses at the front and rear of the ride. If you have a young or nervous horse in the group, put a quiet one on the outside to shield him from the traffic, but never ride more than two abreast. It is safer not to have too many riders in the group – a maximum of ten would be a sensible number – otherwise the leading and rear files lose sight of each other. There should always be an experienced rider both at the front and back of the ride who is responsible for keeping the group together and for giving clear signals to the other road users.

If you have to cross the road, ensure that there is plenty of time for everyone to cross together; if not, wait until the road is clear. Stable mates often make a fuss if separated. Do not rely on someone else to thank considerate motorists : it is better that everyone should do it than that nobody should.

The leader must ensure that he is setting a pace that everyone can maintain with ease. If there are inexperienced riders in the group, their permission should be sought before he increases it. If a horse does get out of control, the whole ride must be stopped immediately. In nine cases out of ten, the runaway will slow up of his own accord when he realises that his companions are not with him. Never chase a horse that has bolted : you will only make him go faster. The only thing you can do is to stand still and hope that the rider will be able to get him under control.

Horses bolt very rarely, but when they do it is usually for one of three main reasons : fear, over-excitement or pain. If a horse is really terrified, he is blind to all reason, and must be stopped by any means in the rider's power. This is the one occasion when consideration for the horse's mouth can be forgotten. It is useless, however, to lean back and pull on the reins with both hands at the same time – the horse will only fight against you. If he bolts on the road, try to pull his head into the hedge as quickly as possible. If you are in a field, pull hard on one rein only and try to bring him round in a decreasing circle. You can usually feel if a horse is getting beyond your control, so try to stop him before he gathers speed by a give-and-take action of your hands. Shorten the reins, then pull hard and immediately give with your hands again. A little of this treatment will often surprise the horse into slowing up. Speak quietly to him all the time to try and calm him down. If he is over-excited, he will probably be more responsive than if he is in a blind panic, and more gentle handling will quite often be sufficient.

If he is trying to escape pain from badly fitted tack, or because the rider's rough hands are bruising his mouth, then the solution is obvious. A great number of horses develop into chronic pullers solely because the rider is always pulling against them; hard-handed riders will inevitably produce hard-mouthed horses.

If you are unfortunate enough to fall off, you have to make a quick decision as to whether or not to hang on to the reins. If the horse is galloping and you find yourself falling, let go of the reins and roll out of his way as quickly as possible. In these circumstances, by holding on to the reins you would be dragged along the ground and would risk further injury. On the other hand, if the horse is going slowly and merely shies at something or suddenly stops, causing you to lose your balance, and the fall is quite a simple one, then try to prevent the horse from galloping off by keeping a hold on the reins – a loose horse in a crowd is always a danger.

Riding on slippery roads

Ride very cautiously on any slippery surface. It is safer to take your feet out of the stirrups temporarily, so that if the horse falls you will not be in danger of getting your legs trapped underneath him.

If you are riding on an icy road, it is safer to get off and lead the horse. Don't try to keep him on his feet by holding his head up, as he will find it easier to balance if he has the freedom of his head and neck. Ride as close to the edge of the road as possible; there is more likely to be grit or dirt there which will help to provide a footing.

If you have to exercise in snow, pick the horse's feet out, and smear motor grease thickly on the soles, to prevent the snow from balling in the hooves.

Riding at night or in fog

Never ride at night if you can avoid it. There is bound to be a certain amount of risk, even if you are an experienced rider and take every precaution. Drivers cannot always be relied upon to dip their headlights, and sudden shadows can be unnerving to the most placid of horses. If, however, you are obliged to take your horse out at night, make sure that you can be clearly seen.

Your local Road Safety Officer will advise you on the most effective clothing that you can wear. The Royal Society for the Prevention of Accidents has produced a range of fluorescent and reflective garments, tabards, armbands etc, as well as reflective bandages that can be worn by the horse. You can also buy stirrup safety lights which show a white light to the front and a red one to the rear.

If you are caught unprepared in the dark or in a thick fog, tie a white handkerchief to your right arm or stirrup. If you are coming home from hunting, untie your stock and wind that round your arm.

To be correctly equipped when riding in a group, the leader should wear a light showing white to the front, and the rider at the back should wear one showing red to the rear. If neither lamps nor reflective clothing are available, then place the lightest coloured horses to the front and rear.

Leading a horse on the road

When leading a horse, either on foot or from another horse, keep to the left-hand side of the road and lead from your left hand, placing yourself between the led horse and the traffic. Most people find it awkward to lead from their left hand, and the horse too will be unaccustomed to it, so it would be wise to practise before you go out. If leading at night and on foot, carry a light in your outside hand.

Never lead a horse on a busy road with a headcollar only; if he tried to pull away, you would have very little control. When leading with a bridle, take the reins over the horse's head so that you have a longer rein with which to control him. If you are leading a young or nervous horse, it is safer to attach a long leading rein or lunge to the bit and dispense with the reins, as this will give you more scope if he plays up or tries to get away. To prevent the bit from being pulled sideways through the mouth, you can use a special attachment called a New-market chain, which can be bought at any saddler's. This is a short, branched chain which is attached to each ring of the

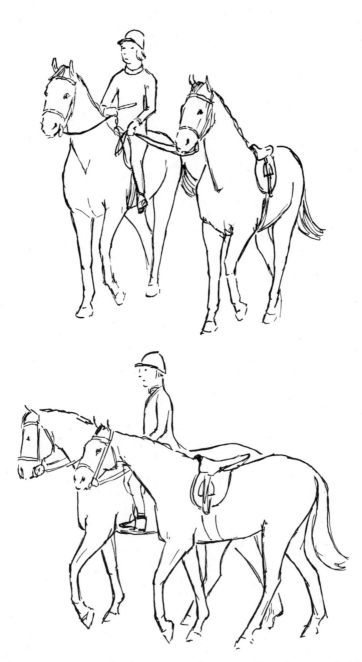

The correct way to lead one horse from another : front and side
views

How to secure the run-up stirrups on the led horse to prevent them from slipping down

bit and affords an even pull on the mouth. Never wrap the spare end around your hand; it could be trapped if the horse pulls suddenly.

Be very careful when passing pedestrians – give them a wide berth, as some may be frightened of horses. When you are riding one horse and leading another, make sure the led horse has plenty of room when passing stationary cars or cyclists. If the led horse is wearing a saddle, secure the stirrups as shown below to prevent them from sliding down the leathers.

4

Riding in
the Country

There is something very satisfying about viewing the countryside from the back of a horse. The charm of a quiet ride through a wood, or the exhilaration of a gallop across open moorland on a well-mannered, well-loved horse, can probably only be fully understood by those who have experienced it.

It is a wonderful opportunity to learn about the countryside, crops and animals, particularly if you intend to go hunting. For example, during your ride you can learn to recognise the difference between oats, wheat and barley, or between meadow hay and clover. How many breeds of cattle can you distinguish? Do you know what the various farm implements are used for? If you are observant you can catch glimpses of all kinds of wildlife. The list is endless, and if you live in a town, a ride in the country provides the means of getting into closer touch with rural life.

It is also a first-class schooling ground for your horse. You can get him accustomed to other animals – some horses are terrified of pigs! Even the smell of a farmyard will upset a nervous horse. Occasionally he will refuse to go past a certain place, not because he can see something that frightens him, but because there is a strange smell. Many horses fear the smell of blood and will refuse to go anywhere near an abattoir. Getting him used to a variety of sights, sounds and smells is all part of a horse's education.

Responsibilities of a country ride

It is important to remember that riding in the countryside entails extra discipline and a sense of responsibility. Some riders, who have perhaps been brought up in towns, upset the farmers through ignorance of country ways.

Always respect other people's property; never ride on private land without permission. A farmer who bans all riders from his land has probably done so because of some previous bad behaviour on their part. Never jump fences unless invited, and keep away from growing crops.

Remember to close gates behind you, and make absolutely sure that they are latched securely. Keep strictly to bridle paths where requested; footpaths are for pedestrians only.

When riding past farmyards, or fields in which horses or cattle are grazing, ride slowly. If you hurry, you may excite the animals and cause them to start galloping. Do not allow your horse to stop and sniff at another over a gate or hedge – not only will the other horse be encouraged to jump out, but he may have a cough which could be infectious. Never ride across a field in which other horses are grazing, as there is likely to be a stampede.

If you meet another rider, give him plenty of room to pass. Horses that are strangers to each other are liable to kick. If you stop to talk, don't allow your horses to sniff each other; this also may result in a kicking match. When overtaking another rider or group of riders, go slowly, and keep an eye on the horses to make sure you are not upsetting them.

When crossing a river or ford, do not allow your horse to stand still, as he may try to lie down in the water. He will usually give you a warning if he intends to do so by pawing at it first. It is safer to take your feet out of the stirrups when crossing boggy ground or deep water; this way you are less likely to get caught under the horse if he falls.

When riding down a steep slope, keep your horse straight; if you ride diagonally his legs are more likely to slip from under him. Resist the temptation to lean backwards; your body should remain at right angles to the horse. In this way you will be sitting over his centre of gravity and he will find it easier to keep his balance.

Never throw lighted cigarette ends away. Carelessness in this respect, especially during a dry period, could lead to a disastrous fire. Also, if you are eating sandwiches, keep the wrappings in your pocket; plastic bags are dangerous if eaten by animals, and in addition, litter in the countryside is just as deplorable as in the towns.

Opening and closing gates

Always take great care when opening or closing a gate to ensure that the horse has plenty of room to walk through without hitting himself on the gate post. You should learn how to do it without dismounting, but if the catch is difficult it is safer to get off.

To open a gate successfully while still mounted, make your horse stand parallel to it, facing the latch. Undo the catch, and either push the gate away or pull it towards you as the case may be. (Here a well-trained horse is a great advantage, as he will move sideways away from your leg in whichever direction you wish.) Walk through quietly, then turn your horse round and, standing parallel to the gate again, either push or pull it shut. Be careful, when leaning forward to fasten the catch, that the horse doesn't catch his bit or reins in it. Some horses will fidget while the rider is trying to open or close a gate; it may take a lot of time and patience to cure them, but they must be taught to stand still.

If you go through in front of others, make sure that the gate does not swing back and hit another horse. When someone opens a gate for you, stand quite still until he has latched it securely; if your horse is moving around, he will have difficulty in keeping his own horse still.

Wise precautions

If you are going on a long ride, the following could come in useful in an emergency : money for the telephone, hoofpick, string, penknife and a bandage. If your horse suddenly goes lame, dismount immediately and inspect his foot – he has probably picked up a stone.

When you set out on your ride, it is a sensible idea to let someone know in which direction you intend to go. If you are unfortunate enough to have a fall, and your horse gallops home riderless, at least there will be somebody with an idea as to where you might be.

After your ride

Never bring the horse into the stable while he is sweating. Let him walk quietly for the last mile so that he has time to dry off and to enter the stable in a relaxed frame of mind. If he is still sweating, make sure he is thoroughly dry before you leave him, otherwise he will be liable to catch a chill.

Some people advocate leaving the saddle on for ten minutes, with the girths loosened, in order to allow the back to cool down gradually. In theory this is probably a good idea, but in practice the horse will be likely to roll and smash the saddle unless he is either tied up or supervised. If you ease the saddle off gently, and give the back a good rub with your hand to restore the circulation, no harm will be done by removing it.

Remember to give the horse a drink before you feed him. (This is discussed more fully on p. 72.)

One final plea. If your horse misbehaves on the ride and your temper is aroused, never take it out on him when he comes back to the stable. He will have no idea why he is being chastised. I once heard a man say, because his horse had consistently refused to jump a small fence, 'I shut 'un up in 'is box, and gave 'un a damn good 'ammering!' Such mindlessness is hard to believe.

5

Make your Stable Safe

Not many people can afford to have a stable built to their own design; most of us have to be content with an existing building, or with having an old one converted. Nevertheless, whichever type you acquire there are some fundamental aspects of safety which should always be considered. The first questions one should ask are 'Is the stable free of all hazards? Are there any danger points, or anything on which the horse could hurt himself? Is it big enough for the size of the horse, and high enough to prevent him from hitting his head?' A horse that is stabled for twenty-three hours out of twenty-four is apt to get bored, and will start looking round for diversions such as chewing wood, pawing, or kicking at the walls or partitions. Your stable doesn't have to be smart, but it is essential that it is safe.

The site

Of course, if you already have your building there is little you can do about its site, but if you are erecting one the choice of position is most important. Try to find a plot of ground with good natural drainage, preferably at the top of a slight slope so that the water does not accumulate around the stable in the winter. If possible build on light sandy soil, as this will be drier than heavy clay. There must be some kind of protection from cold north winds, and ideally the stable should face south so that the horse can get the maximum benefit from the sun.

Remember that a stabled horse needs attention at least three times a day (the minimum number of times he will have to be fed), so your building must be at a convenient distance from your home, and also must have easy access for supply lorries and the removal of manure. It must, of course, have water readily available, as a horse will drink anything from four to ten gallons per day.

Building materials

The material you use is a matter of personal preference, cost and availability, always bearing in mind that the building must be strong, durable and safe. A brick-built stable would be ideal, but the cost of bricks may be prohibitive, and concrete blocks make a very good substitute. Probably the cheapest solution is to buy one of the modern, portable stables made of wood. These can either be erected for you by the manufacturer, or sent with 'do-it-yourself' instructions for you to put up. A word of warning, though: unless you have had experience of building, it could pay in the long run to have a professional builder to erect the stable – your mistakes may prove even more costly! For example, unless the foundation is absolutely level, you may find after a while that your building is beginning to warp.

You will need not only a stable, of course, but also somewhere to store food and tack. The portable stables can be bought with or without a tack room attached. In the interests of safety, hay should be stored away from the stable so that, in the event of fire, the horse would not be at risk.

You may find that your horse takes a liking to new wood, and will start chewing it. A liberal coating of creosote will help to prevent this, and will also preserve the wood. There are in addition other preventatives, available from any saddler's, which discourage a horse from chewing wooden gates, fences, partitions, rugs, bandages, reins etc.

Size

The size of your loose-box will, of course, depend on the size of your horse. The standard boxes are 14ft × 12ft (4.2m × 3.6m) for a horse of about 15.2hh or over, but a pony will be perfectly comfortable in a smaller one 12ft × 10ft (3.6m × 3m). These sizes are generous, and will give the animal plenty of room in which to move round.

The ceiling must be high enough to ensure that the horse cannot hit his head if he rears, and to allow plenty of room for the circulation of air. Some of the old-fashioned boxes with low hanging beams are dangerous.

Floors and drainage

The materials used for floors are as varied as those used for the building of the stable itself, and they all have advantages and drawbacks. The important factors are that they should be non-slip, long-lasting and impervious to moisture.

Wooden floors are not advisable as they will rot and splinter unless kept absolutely dry. *Cement* and *concrete* are longer-lasting, but must be kept roughened on the surface, otherwise they become slippery. Ordinary *bricks* are rather porous, and wear unevenly, but are not slippery.

In many stables overseas, particularly in America, floors are made of *clay* or *hard-packed earth*, which is warm but difficult to keep clean.

Probably the best flooring material is *Staffordshire brick*, which is grooved on the upper surface, non-slip, and long-lasting; but it is expensive.

As you can see, the choice is yours, but whichever material you decide on, success will depend on your own diligence and horsemastership. If the floor is not kept scrupulously clean, the stable will become a health hazard. Not only do decomposing manure and urine provide a breeding ground for bacteria and germs, but the ammonia which is given off in the air is an irritant to the eyes and lungs of a horse.

There is no need to go to the expense of having a complicated drainage system installed; a gentle slope outwards is all that is required. The bedding itself will provide ample drainage, as long as the damp portions are removed daily. The slope towards the door should be minimal, otherwise there would be a certain amount of strain on the horse's legs.

A central drain in the middle of the box, with a removable cover, is not to be recommended for two main reasons. The first is that it soon becomes blocked, especially if sawdust is used for bedding; and secondly, the horse may crack the grid and could get his foot trapped.

Bedding

There are many different types of bedding, but whichever is used it is essential that the horse has an adequate supply. It is false economy to skimp on bedding material. If the horse is forced to lie on a bare floor, he will be liable to knock his joints, resulting in the swellings known as 'big knees', 'capped hocks' or 'capped elbows'.

Wheat straw is generally accepted as the best type of bedding: it affords good drainage, is sweet-smelling, makes a warm comfortable bed, and is easily disposed of as manure. *Oat straw* is more easily available in some parts of the country, but as it is more palatable, some horses are inclined to eat it. *Barley straw* is less satisfactory as the awns on the ears are prickly and can be irritating, particularly to horses with sensitive skins.

Other forms of bedding are sawdust, peat, shavings and sand. *Sawdust* and *peat*, unless kept absolutely dry and clean, are apt to ball up in the horse's feet and cause rotting if not picked out regularly, and there is always a certain amount dropped from the feet which spoils a tidy yard. *Shavings* make quite a good bed, but unless carefully raked over may contain chips of wood or nails that could injure the horse. *Sand* may be cheap, but if it is sea-sand the horse is inclined to lick it, as it contains salt, and if swallowed in any quantity it will cause colic.

Cost and availability will no doubt influence you in your choice, but whichever type of bedding you use, provided it is kept clean, dry and sweet-smelling, and the floor is kept thickly covered both day and night, your horse will be protected from injury.

Some people like to take up the bedding during the day to give the floor an airing, but in my view this is a mistake. Most horses will not stale (spend a penny) on a hard surface where they are likely to splash their legs, and also they will not be encouraged to lie down. A contented horse who lies down frequently will ease his legs and help to prevent them from 'filling' (swelling through stagnation of the blood). Additionally, he is less likely to pick up bad stable habits such as weaving (swinging the head from side to side), wind-sucking (swallowing air by drawing his head into his chest) or crib-biting (getting hold of the manger or some other projection with his teeth, arching his neck, and swallowing air). Some horses will chew the wood of doors and mangers out of sheer boredom.

Ventilation

The subjects of ventilation and drainage are closely connected. Unless the stable is kept scrupulously clean, the air is bound to be affected by the foul emanations from decomposing manure. It is essential for the preservation of health, especially if a number of horses are kept under one roof, that the air should be pure and plentiful. If you find the walls of the stable dripping with condensation overnight, your horses are being kept in an unhealthy atmosphere.

It is a mistake to think that a warm stable is beneficial to the horse. Germs will breed in a hot atmosphere, increasing the risk of coughs and colds. A close, muggy stable also has a detrimental effect on the lungs. It may be interesting to learn that in Russia, where the winters are many degrees colder than in this country, it has been proved that horses kept in well-ventilated, cool stables are much healthier than those shut up in warm but airless conditions, where the difference in temperature when they go outside could be as much as 44°C.

As the weather gets colder, instead of closing all the doors, add more clothing, and keep the horse's legs warm by applying stable bandages (see pp. 76–8). If the stable is fairly sheltered, your horse will come to no harm if the top half of the stable door is left open day and night, both summer and winter – unless, of course, rain is blowing in, or there is a gale.

To test the warmth of a horse, feel his ears. If they are cold, he needs an extra rug or blanket.

Good ventilation, of course, should not imply draughts. A stream of cold air playing on a horse's back is liable to produce a chill, and swollen legs are often the result of a continuous draught coming in under the stable door.

Windows

If you are designing your own stable, the ideal windows to have are the louvered type which admit air in an upward direction rather than directly on to the horse. They must be on the same side as the door in order to prevent a cross-draught. Make sure all windows are protected by a grille or iron bars to stop the horse from poking his nose through them.

Doors

Ideally, stable doors should always be in two halves, not only to ensure good ventilation but also to allow the horse to look out and take an interest in what is going on. It is very bad for any horse to be shut away on his own; this is particularly true of the young animal who, if shut up, is denied the opportunity of becoming used to everyday sights and sounds. Always ensure that the top half of the door is tied back securely : a swinging door could give a horse a nasty bang on the head.

The doorway itself should be wide enough to allow plenty of clearance as the horse walks in and out. Once a horse has knocked himself, he may either refuse to enter, or start rushing through the doorway – a habit which could become dangerous.

Doors should always open outwards for easy access. A door which opens inwards not only disturbs the bedding, but is impossible to open if a horse should be unfortunate enough to get cast against it. ('Getting cast' is the expression used when a horse rolls over and is unable to get up again because his legs are too close to the wall and there is no room for him to put them on the ground.) Some stables have walls which are specially grooved so that the horse can get a foothold and push himself away from the wall.

A cast horse

Always have two bolts on the bottom door, one at the top and another lower down where the horse cannot reach it. Some horses are adept at undoing catches and letting themselves out.

Electric fittings

Make sure that all light switches are either out of reach of the horse or fitted with guards. Light bulbs must be encased in metal grilles, which should be removable so that the bulb can be cleaned occasionally. Dusty bulbs can become overheated, and could well start a fire if allowed to touch hay or straw.

All electric wiring should be checked regularly, and fixed firmly where it cannot be chewed or stepped on by the horse.

Mangers

There are many different designs of manger, and numerous opinions as to the suitability of each type. Some people argue that it is more natural for a horse to feed from ground level, while others maintain that there are disadvantages; but whichever method is adopted, it must be with the safety of the horse in mind.

The chief objection to feeding from receptacles on the ground is that the horse can knock them over and get them entangled round his feet. Some horses are inclined to paw when feeding, and no matter how sturdy the feed tin is, they will manage to get a foot in it. Also it has to be removed after each feed, which is not always convenient.

A manger fixed to the wall is undoubtedly safer, but the space underneath must be blocked in so that the horse cannot hit his knees on it or become cast underneath it when lying down. A point worth remembering here is to have the manger on the same side as the door, or at least near it. Horses are inclined to get fidgety when feeding, and are liable to lash out if you have to walk past them in order to get out of the box.

Avoid the type of old-fashioned manger that has an inbuilt space for water adjoining the feed portion; horses will invariably slobber water on to their feed, and drop mouthfuls of food into the water. For this reason, water should be kept well away from the manger.

Water

If possible, horses should have access to water at all times. The obvious way to ensure this would be to instal self-filling water bowls, but this is not practical in most cases because of the expense. Another disadvantage is that you will have no idea how much your horse is drinking, and as water is vital to his health, this is an important factor.

The alternative is to keep a filled bucket in the box. Some well-behaved horses never knock their buckets over, and any strongly made wooden, rubber or plastic bucket, placed in the corner of the box and well packed round with bedding, will be adequate for them. However, every stable seems to have its 'Just William', who delights in picking up everything that moves and flinging it around the box for fun. This type of playboy should have his bucket fixed to the wall by a strong hook or bracket of such a design that there is no sharp point on which he could injure himself.

Ensure that the bucket is scrubbed out regularly, as it quickly becomes slimy and coated with grime.

Haynets

An economical and safe way to feed hay is from a net tied to a ring in the wall. Make sure it is tied high enough to prevent the horse from getting a foot caught in it if he pawed. Remember that as the net empties it will drop a little lower; to counteract this, slip the drawstring through one of the lower meshes and pull up tightly. As an additional safety precaution, and also to save yourself time undoing the knot, secure with a quick-release knot.

Hay can be fed from the floor, but this is wasteful, as the horse treads a lot of it into the bedding, and it cannot be weighed as easily as in a net.

The old-fashioned type of hay rack that is usually fixed high up on the wall is not recommended : it forces the horse to eat from an unnatural level, and hayseeds tend to fall into his eyes.

The dangers of an untidy stable

Always be on the lookout for anything in the stable that could injure the horse. Projecting nails, sharp edges, bits of string left lying around (plastic string is particularly dangerous, as it will not dissolve if swallowed), plastic bags, barbed wire, broken glass – the list is endless, and calls for constant vigilance.

Untidy people are a menace in any stable yard. For example, a stable fork left lying on the ground could pierce a leg and ruin a horse for life. Get into the habit of tidiness. Never leave grooming utensils on the floor of the box, or items of tack or tools all over the yard. Close doors securely, especially the one to the feed room. If a horse broke in, he could literally 'eat himself to death'; a surfeit of oats can kill. Although horses are generally fussy eaters, they will sometimes chew reins or any tack that may be hanging near enough for them to reach.

Keep all foodstuffs in vermin-proof containers, and check hay regularly to make sure that it is not heating. If hay is stored when it is damp, it can self-ignite. Stack it away from the stable if possible.

When you are dealing with the public, as in a riding school, safety precautions must be even more stringent. A tidy well-organised yard will help to diminish accidents, while a stable that has no rules, and allows everyone to do more or less as he likes, will be at risk.

Fire precautions

The most horrifying thing that can happen in any yard is a bad fire. Quite recently a survey was done in America which showed that, over a five-year period, there had been 29,000 stable fires. The most common causes were heaters, faulty electric wiring, careless smoking, arson, children playing with matches, and spontaneous ignition of hay. Most of these could have been avoided with a little extra care.

No Smoking notices should be pinned up in prominent positions, and the rule strictly enforced. Fire buckets with sand/water, and fire extinguishers, should be placed within easy reach, and personnel taught how to use them. An occasional fire-drill practice could save time in an emergency. The telephone numbers of the fire station, vet and doctor should be put up on a board where everyone can see them. If the fire engine is called, send someone to meet it so that it can be directed to the fire as quickly as possible.

Most horses are terrified of fire and could be difficult to lead out of the stable. If your horse refuses to move, throw a coat over his head, or tie a towel or cloth around his eyes, and speak quietly to him to reassure him. Be careful not to cover his nostrils, as he must have plenty of air.

Try to ensure against fire by checking all electrical appliances regularly; by forbidding anyone to smoke in the stable; by checking the temperature of the hay and also the manure heap (this too can become hot); and by storing the hay away from the stable building.

Always check stabled horses last thing at night.

6

Stable Routine

Whenever you work around horses, do so quietly and calmly. Your safety depends on your own behaviour. Sudden movements or loud noises will upset a horse and put him on edge. You may think that this is being unnecessarily fussy, but later on when you are able to deal with young horses, and may perhaps have one of your own to break in, you will understand why it is so important to get into good habits. As I have already mentioned, making a mistake with an older horse may be tolerated, but with a young one it could have disastrous results.

A stabled horse is being kept in unnatural conditions, and it will need all your expertise, common sense and hard work to keep him healthy and good-tempered. By looking after him yourself, you will get to know his habits and idiosyncrasies and be able to build up a mutual trust. You will have to learn how to feed, groom and bandage him, check his shoes and teeth, and do many other things in which safety plays a major part.

Grooming

Horses that are kept in the stable must be groomed in order to keep their skin in good condition, tone up the muscles, improve the circulation and give a healthy gloss to the coat. If you have never groomed a horse, it is essential that you learn by demonstration; the following is merely a rough outline of the procedure and of some of the precautions that should be taken.

The tools you will need are:
Hoofpick: metal hook used for cleaning out feet.
Dandy brush: has stiff bristles; used to remove mud and sweat.
Curry comb: if made of metal, used *only to clean body brush*; if made of rubber or nylon, can be used to remove dirt and loose hair from coat.

Body brush: has short soft hairs, and is used to groom the coat of a stabled horse, particularly one that is clipped. Also used on manes and tails.

Wisp: made of hay twisted into a rope, which is then made into a hard pad. Used for 'banging' (developing and hardening muscles).

Sponge for eyes and nose: used for cleaning them out.

Sponge for dock: used for cleaning underneath tail and rectal area.

Water brush: soft-haired narrow brush, used in 'laying' the mane (damping it and brushing it neatly over to one side).

Mane comb: metal comb used for 'pulling' (shortening and thinning mane), and for improving the shape and appearance of the top of the tail.

Bucket of water: used for laying mane, washing hooves etc.

Sweat scraper: made of metal on one side and rubber on the other. Not used during normal grooming, but only to scrape off sweat, or water, if horse has been out in rain.

Stable rubber: used to give coat final polish.

Each item is used for a specific purpose, and great damage can be inflicted if their uses are not fully understood, or if they are handled carelessly.

The ideal time to groom is immediately after exercise, when the horse is still warm. His pores are then open and the scurf and dirt will rise to the surface. To begin, ensure that all your grooming tools are collected together in a box or container of some kind, and that they are clean and in good condition. Next, tie the horse up with a fairly short lead rope so that he cannot wander round the box or nip you while you are grooming.

For your own safety, do not make any hasty or sudden movements; a horse is easily startled, and you may frighten him if you knock him with the brush or drop your tools with a clatter. Be particularly careful when grooming his head, eyes and ears: if you are too rough you will make him head-shy. Also take care when grooming his hind legs; always start from the quarters and gradually work down over the legs.

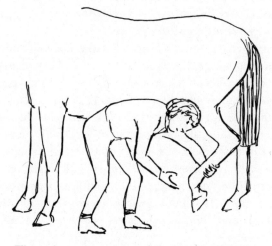

The safe way to pick up the horse's hind leg

Before you start to brush him, his feet must be picked out with a hoofpick. Always remember to speak to the horse before picking up a hind leg, and make sure that you run your hand down over the quarters before placing it on the leg. The hoof pick should be used in the direction of heel to toe; in this way the dirt will be thrown away from the heel, and there will be no risk of accidentally piercing the soft part of the frog with the pick. Hold the horse's leg in a comfortable position, so that he can balance easily on three legs. If you hold the foot over a dung skep (basket used to remove droppings), or any convenient receptacle, you will keep the bedding clean.

After picking out the feet, you can proceed with the actual grooming. On an unclipped horse, you may first use the dandy brush or rubber curry comb to remove sweat marks, mud and loose hair. The dandy is much too harsh to be used on an animal that is clipped, or on any of the tender parts of the horse, such as the head or the areas around the eyes or between the hind legs. Begin on the neck, and work with the lay of the hair. The head should be left until last, when you will have to remove the headcollar and use only the soft body brush.

The body brush is the most important coat cleaner, and if used in long sweeping strokes will get down to the base of the hair and remove all the dirt and scurf.

The wisp, which is made from hay twisted into a rope, is used as a form of massage. There is an art to making one correctly, and it is quite difficult to accomplish, so ask some knowledgeable person to show you how it is done. It is used primarily to develop the muscles of a horse which is being got fit for racing, hunting or eventing, by being brought vigorously down with a bang on the muscles of the neck, quarters, and thighs. Avoid the loin area (just behind the saddle), as you might damage the kidneys which lie underneath; also avoid any bony prominences or tender regions. It is not necessary to use the wisp during the course of ordinary grooming unless you want to make your horse extra fit.

Having groomed the horse, his eyes and nose must be gently wiped with the sponge, which is kept scrupulously clean for the purpose. With a second sponge, clean under the dock and around the rectal area in a similar manner. If you use sponges of different colours you will always be able to distinguish between the two.

To complete the grooming process, lay the mane : that is, dip the water brush lightly in water, and brush the mane on to the off side of the neck, working from the roots downwards.

Finish off by giving the coat a final polish with the stable rubber. If you want to look extra smart, and at the same time help to prevent the horse's feet from becoming brittle, paint the hooves with hoof oil.

'Pulling' mane and tail

If the mane is too thick and long, it can be thinned and shortened by pulling the hairs out with a mane comb. It needs quite a lot of skill to pull a mane correctly, and if you are inexperienced you should only do it under supervision. Never pull too much hair out at one time as you will make the horse's neck sore. Make sure that all the loose hair is carefully collected, and not left lying around in the straw where it could be picked up and eaten. If it gets into the horse's stomach, it can ball up and cause a stoppage.

Tail pulling is done in a similar manner, to improve the appearance of the top of the tail, but should not be attempted by the novice. Never clip or cut the hair at the top of the tail with scissors; when it begins to grow out, it will stick out like the bristles of a brush.

Clipping

It may seem odd that a horse is clipped (has his coat mechanically removed) in the winter, when the weather is at its coldest. Not all horses, of course, need to be clipped – only those required to do fast work, such as hunters, eventers, racehorses etc. During the winter a horse grows a heavy coat – some are much thicker than others – and if he is doing a lot of fast work he will sweat profusely, causing him distress and loss of condition. If his coat is short, he will dry more quickly, and therefore be less likely to catch a chill; he will be easier to groom, and will not lose weight because of excessive sweating.

If you intend to hunt your horse, the best time to clip would be in October, before the foxhunting season begins. The different types of clip are as follows :

Hunter clip. Body is clipped all over, but hair is left on legs and a patch under the saddle (shaped to fit saddle). Hair on legs will help to protect against thorns, mud, knocks and chills. Hair under saddle will provide a cushion to protect back from soreness and injury.
Full clip. Horse is clipped all over, including legs and saddle patch. Makes grooming and drying of legs and back easier, but affords no protection to either.
Trace clip. Coat is removed from belly – to the height of the traces if the horse was pulling a cart, hence the name – and up underneath the neck to the throat. Legs left unclipped. This clip can be used on horses that are not hunted regularly, but are kept

at grass and turned out in a New Zealand rug (see pp. 83–4). Personally, I dislike this method, as the horse must feel the cold round the belly region in spite of the rug, especially on a bitter winter's night.

Blanket clip. Similar to trace clip, but coat is also removed from head, neck and shoulders, leaving a patch resembling a blanket. Horses with this clip should be stabled at night.

Never attempt to clip a horse on your own if you have had little experience. It is a job which requires great skill, and there must be a knowledgeable person to help you. Some horses are nervous of the noise and sensation of a clipper, and you could get into a dangerous situation.

Make sure your clipper blades are sharp, clean, and well oiled. (Dipping them in kerosene will ensure cleanliness, but they must be thoroughly dried. To oil the machine you can use any sewing-machine oil.) The tension of the blades is very important. It must be tight enough to clip, but not so tight that the blades become hot. Obviously the plug must be well earthed to prevent an electric shock, which has been known to happen through carelessness. As an additional safety precaution, wear rubber soled boots or shoes. Make sure too that the horse cannot chew or step on the lead.

It is likely to take at least an hour to clip a horse successfully if he has a full or hunter clip.

The horse's coat must be absolutely dry and clean. Never clip after exercise – the coat may be slightly damp and the blades will not cut satisfactorily.

Allow the clippers to run for a few minutes, holding them away from the horse, so that he becomes accustomed to the noise, and then gradually begin clipping. Start on the shoulder or neck, against the lie of the hair, and do not force the blades forward too quickly or you will drag the hair. Make sure also that they are flat and not cutting into the skin. Do not clip the hair on the inside of the ears – this is there for protection against insects, dirt, cold etc.

If you are doing a hunter clip, the shape of the saddle can be marked by tracing round the saddle with a piece of chalk.

Be extra careful when clipping ticklish or tender parts, such as around the girth and elbow areas or near the hind legs.

It is advisable to leave the head until last, as some horses object to having clippers on their heads and cannot be clipped without assistance. It may be necessary to put on a 'twitch' (a wooden handle with a loop of rope at one end). This is looped around the upper lip and twisted so that the lip is held firm. It is not necessary to twist so hard that you cause the horse pain; just pull it tight enough to make him keep his head still. This works with most horses, but be prepared for yours to fight; if he does, the twitch is too tight and must be loosened.

Great care must be taken when clipping around the eyes and ears. Be prepared for any sudden movement that the horse might make; an accidental slip could do serious damage. Also be careful when clipping near the mane, as you may cut a chunk off unintentionally.

When doing his head, throw a rug over the horse's body to prevent a chill.

Feeding and exercise

The whole art of good stable management lies in the correct balance between feeding and exercise. It is important to learn about the effect that different foods can have on the behaviour of your horse, and both for his safety and yours you would be advised to seek help from an experienced person who knows your particular animal, his temperament, the amount of work he is required to do, and so on. Each horse is an individual, and it would be just as misleading to attempt to advise a diet for an unknown horse as it would be to tell you what you should eat yourself!

Nevertheless, there are some general comments that can be made, and a few accepted rules that should be understood and followed in the interests of health and safety.

Before man interfered with the natural eating habits of the

horse, he was entirely a grazing animal, and kept himself alive by eating only when it suited him. He ate little at a time, but grazed often. His comparatively small stomach prevented him from digesting large quantities. By studying the habits of his ancestors, we can adjust our present system of feeding to keep it as close to nature's way as possible. One of the first rules, then, should be to feed little and often. Ideally, a horse should be fed four times a day, with the biggest feed being given at night when he has plenty of time to digest it. If this is not practical, then it must be at least three times, if he is stabled all the time.

It is important to feed according to the work the horse is required to do, and any stabled horse must have at least one hour's exercise per day, and two or three if being prepared for eventing or racing. As I have mentioned before, lack of exercise and too much food is a dangerous combination, particularly if the food is oats. The 'safe' foods are hay and bran, inasmuch as they do not have an exciting effect on a horse, but at the same time they are unable to build strength and muscle without additions such as oats. Never gallop or work a horse hard on a full stomach; it will impair his wind and may give him colic. Rest him for at least an hour after a feed.

His diet should not be changed suddenly. For example, if you have been giving him a lot of hard food such as oats, barley or maize, he must not be turned out into a field of lush grass – a dose of colic would almost certainly be the result. However, a short spell in the field as frequently as you can manage, or as weather permits, during the winter months, will do him good both physically and mentally, as the grass is minimal and not too rich.

If water is available all the time, the horse will not drink too much at any one time, but if it is not, always water before a feed. If he drinks a large amount after eating, the food will be washed undigested out of the stomach.

It is important that only good-quality forage is fed. Mouldy hay, or dusty dry food, will have a detrimental effect on both wind and stomach. Always remove any stale food from the manger before feeding, particularly mashes, as they soon become sour.

A horse needs a certain amount of salt in his diet; to ensure that he gets it, either provide a salt lick or add a teaspoonful to his feed once a day.

There is a great deal to be learnt about feeding horses, and lack of knowledge can lead to dangerous mistakes. Safety lies in seeking advice before it is too late.

Suitable foods

It is not possible within the scope of this book to go into too much detail on the subject of feeding, but the following are some of the points that should be borne in mind, and some of the dangers that can be avoided.

Hay

Hay is the most natural food that a horse can be given. It gives him the bulk he needs to promote good digestion, and no harm can be done by giving him too much – except perhaps by making him too fat – in the case of a greedy feeder.

There are two main types : meadow hay, which is grown on a permanent pasture, and seed hay, which is specially sown. The latter is more nutritious, but meadow hay is softer and more easily digested. Only good-quality hay should be fed; musty, mouldy or dusty hay will harm both lungs and stomach. It should be dry, crisp, sweet-smelling and greenish to light brown in colour.

Oats

Oats are the energy-giving food and staple diet for horses in hard work. If the horse is sick or lame and cannot be exercised, oats should be immediately cut out of his diet. Also stop them if the horse is becoming unmanageable, and substitute slightly damp-ened bran and low-protein horse and pony cubes. Whole oats should be plump and clean. If they are crushed or bruised before feeding, the horse will be able to digest them more easily.

Barley

Whole barley must either be crushed or boiled before feeding. It is a valuable fattening food, but heating if given in too large a quantity. About 1lb (450g), boiled for at least two hours and given with 2–3lb of bran three or four times a week, would probably be sufficient for most horses, but of course it depends on the amount of work the horse is required to do, his size, age, condition etc.

Flaked maize

Maize is also a fattening food, but it adds variety to the diet and often makes a poor feeder eat up.

Horse and pony cubes

These cubes or nuts are a balanced diet in themselves. They vary in content, ranging from the high-protein racehorse nuts to those more suitable for horses and ponies doing less work. Ingredients might include bran, oats, groundnut meal, locust beans, maize, molasses, barley, grass and vitamins.

Although containing almost everything that the horse needs in his diet, these cubes would become monotonous if fed exclusively, but mixed with bran, oats, carrots etc they make an appetising feed. I once worked in a stable in Alaska where the horses were fed on nothing but horse and pony cubes and a very small amount of hay. They all looked in excellent condition, but I could not help feeling how bored they must have been with their meals.

Bran

Bran, which is the husk part of wheat, is a 'safe' food and one of the most useful of all the foodstuffs. It is non-heating, adds bulk to concentrates, and does not have the effect of making a horse too excitable. It also makes an ideal food for sick or lame horses. As it is very dry, it becomes more palatable if slightly dampened before feeding.

A bran mash should be given to horses that are tired, particularly after hunting, as it is easily digested. To make a bran mash, put 3–4lb (1.4–1.8kg) of bran into a stable bucket (about two-thirds of a bucketful), and pour on enough boiling water to damp it through, but not enough to make it wet and sloppy. Stir well, cover with a sack, and allow to steam until cool enough to eat. To make it more appetising, you can add a handful of oats, some sliced carrots, molasses, or boiled linseed.

Linseed

Linseed can be bought either in seed or oil form. It is absolutely essential, if in seed form, that it is boiled thoroughly before being given to a horse. To be on the safe side it is better to soak it all night, then boil for two or three hours. If it is not soaked then it should simmer for three or four hours at least. Unboiled linseed can prove poisonous to a horse, as it contains a type of acid which is detrimental.

Boiled linseed is fed in a bran mash, and is an excellent food for putting weight on a horse and a shine on his coat. Only a little is needed per horse: 4–8oz (110–220g), weighed dry, is ample.

Sugar beet

Sugar beet is another fattening food that adds variety, but it must not be fed in its dry form or it may swell up in the stomach and cause colic. Soak it overnight, and feed while fresh, as it deteriorates rapidly when wet.

Molasses

Molasses is a sweet syrup drained from sugar when it is refined. It can be obtained in dry or liquid form, and makes an excellent appetiser.

Succulent foods

Carrots, mangolds, turnips, apples etc all contain a certain number of vitamins, and make a change from dry food. They are all excellent for horses with poor appetites.

Having said that it is impossible to suggest the exact quantities of the various foods that you should give your horse, the following may give you a rough idea of what a hunter might eat per day if he was perhaps hunting once a week. But remember that this menu may not necessarily be suitable for your own horse in similar circumstances, as his temperament, size, condition etc may be entirely different.

10–12lb (4.5–5.4kg) oats, or mixture of oats and cubes
3lb (1.4kg) bran
12–16lb (5.4–7.3kg) hay
1lb (450g) carrots

These quantities, of course, should be divided into three or four feeds, with only a small amount (5–6lb, or 2.3–2.7kg) of hay in the morning before exercise, and the rest given at night, or after the horse has been exercised. Try to feed something succulent every day, as too much dry food is bad for the horse's digestion.

Bandaging

A great deal of harm can be done to a horse's legs if bandages are not skilfully applied. If they are put on too tightly, they are liable to stop the circulation and injure the tendons at the back of the legs. If too loose, they are ineffective and could cause an accident if the horse became entangled in them.

Bandages have various uses, and there are several different types.

The stable bandage

This can be made of wool, stockinette or flannel, and is used chiefly for warmth and protection. By keeping the legs warm, it increases the circulation and prevents congestion of the blood. Horses that have done a lot of work and then stand for long periods in the stable sometimes suffer from 'filled' legs, and warmth helps to prevent this condition.

The stable bandage is also used to protect the horse's legs

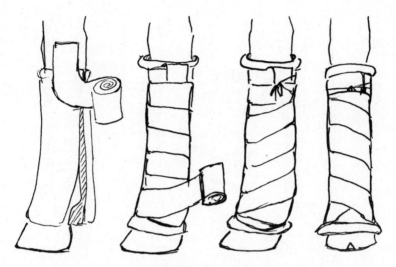

The stable bandage

when travelling, and, with straw underneath, to dry the legs off, if wet or muddy, after exercise or hunting. Except in the latter case, they should always have a layer of cotton wool or gamgee (cotton wool covered by tissue) underneath for extra warmth, and to protect the tendons.

Before commencing to bandage, ensure that the bandage is correctly rolled. The tapes should be on the inside, and the bandage kept taut as it is rolled up. If the roll is too loose, it is difficult to apply evenly. When applying to the leg, do not kneel, but adopt a crouching or stooping position so that you can get out of the way more quickly if the horse moves suddenly.

Start the bandage as shown in the diagram, and ensure that the cotton wool or gamgee covers the coronet (the band at the top of the hoof). This is most important in a travelling bandage, as it helps to protect the coronet from injury. As you unroll, allow the bandage to follow the natural contours of the leg, keeping an even pressure which is firm but not too tight. Tie the tapes in a bow on the outside – not on the front of the leg, where it will press on the cannon bone, nor at the back, where it will press on the tendons. Tie firmly, but not tightly enough to interfere with the circulation, and tuck the spare ends away neatly.

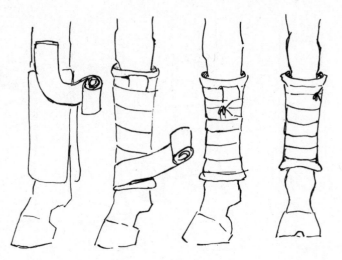

The exercise bandage

A minor point here which may be of interest to people who wish to show their horses. By bandaging the *nearside* legs in an anti-clockwise direction, and the *offside* ones in a clockwise direction, the hair at the back of the leg will be encouraged to point inwards rather than outwards, giving a smoother appearance to the line of the tendons which will please the judge's eye.

The exercise bandage

This is made of stockinette or crêpe, and is used primarily to support the tendons when jumping, and also to protect the legs from knocks, for example when lungeing.

'Exercise bandage' is in fact rather a misnomer, as they are rarely necessary for normal exercising, nor for the average amount of jumping that most horses are required to do. High-class show jumping, of course, is a different matter, as there is much more strain on the horses' legs. If you are in any doubt about your horse's tendons, consult your vet, but if you are inexperienced you can do much more harm to a horse's leg by applying a bandage badly than by not applying one at all. The majority of horses do not need exercise bandages except when being lunged (see chapter 15).

They are applied in the same manner as the stable bandage,

except that they are not extended over the fetlock joint. Be careful that the bandage does not interfere in any way with the mobility of the fetlock joint. If they are worn for jumping, they are generally applied to the forelegs only, as these bear the horse's weight as he lands from a fence.

When bandaging the near leg, it is safer to do so in an anticlockwise direction, and vice versa for the off leg; in this way, if one leg is accidentally hit by the other, particularly while racing, the movement of the leg will be *in the same direction* as the roll of the bandage and will be less likely to work it loose. For extra security, the tape should be stitched where the knot is tied to ensure that it does not come loose.

The tail bandage

Tail bandages are made of stockinette or crêpe, and are narrower than the leg bandages. A great deal of pain and suffering has been caused to horses by inexperienced people putting the tail bandage on too tightly. Crêpe bandages in particular can be dangerous in this respect, and can easily stop the circulation.

They are used to protect the tail when travelling (some horses rub their tails against the back of the box or trailer), or to improve the appearance of the top of the tail, by keeping the hair neat and tidy.

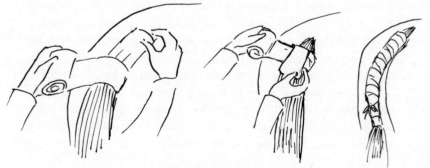

The tail bandage

To apply a tail bandage, first damp the top of the tail with a water brush. This gives the bandage a better grip and keeps the hair lying flat. Never wet the bandage itself, as it may shrink and become too tight. Hold the roll in the right hand, unwind about 8in (20cm) and place this piece underneath the tail. Make one turn, leaving the spare end free, and allow it to fall down over the tail, to be secured by subsequent turns of the bandage. Unroll to near the end of the dock, and tie with the tapes, ensuring that they are not too tight.

Never leave a tail bandage on all night, as there is always a danger that it may be too tight for comfort. To remove it, stand behind the horse (a little to one side to avoid being kicked), grasp the bandage near the top with both hands, and pull gently downwards. There is generally no need to untie the tapes, but if it is proving difficult to pull down, untie them to relieve the tension.

Rugs

There are several different types of rug, each having a specific purpose.

The night rug

This is made of jute or hemp, usually with a woollen lining, and is the most useful article of horse clothing. Its purpose is to keep the horse warm in winter, particularly one that has been clipped. If it is cold, he will probably need one or two blankets underneath for extra warmth. Old army blankets are excellent for this purpose, or any under-rug that can be bought at the saddler's. The horse's ears are quite useful for determining whether or not he is cold. If they are cold to the touch, he needs more clothing. Note also the condition of his coat : if the hair is 'staring' (standing away from the body, rather like a dog's hackles rising), the horse is cold.

The day rug

This is the 'posh' relation of the rug family. It is made of wool, and is usually edged in a braid of a contrasting colour. As its name implies, it is used in the daytime, for travelling, or whenever the horse is required to look extra smart, as at shows.

The anti-sweat rug

This is made of open cotton mesh, rather like a string vest, and is used as a cooler when the horse is sweating. It affords good ventilation, yet keeps the horse warm enough to prevent him from getting a chill. When used underneath the night rug, it helps to prevent a horse from 'breaking out' (breaking into a sweat again after having dried off) by allowing air to circulate under the rug.

The summer sheet

This lightweight cotton sheet is used in the summer to keep the flies off, and also to keep the coat clean.

Rollers and surcingles

A roller is made of leather or webbing, and is padded where it rests on the horse's back to prevent pressure on the spine. It is used to keep the rug in position. There is also an 'anti-cast' roller, with an arched metal bar at the top which prevents the horse from rolling over and becoming cast.

The surcingle is made of webbing, and has no padding. This too is used to keep the rug in place, but you must remember to put a pad underneath – a piece of sheepskin or foam rubber would do – to protect the spine.

Rugging up

Always put on the rug gently, speaking to the horse at the same time. If you suddenly throw it over his back, you will frighten him, particularly if he is young.

Hold it in both hands, at the front, and gently throw it over the neck just in front of the withers. Slide it back into position and do up the buckle at the front. This must be done before the roller is fastened, to prevent the rug from slipping back. Now place the roller on the back just behind the withers, and fasten

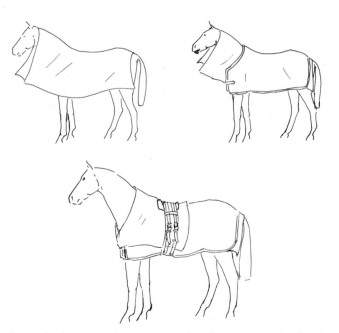

A safe method of securing an underblanket; if the blanket is not long enough to do this, simply turn it back over the front of the rug

it on the near side, firmly but not too tightly. Ensure that the rug is not wrinkled anywhere by running your fingers down between the roller and the rug. It should fit comfortably around the neck without rubbing either the withers or the points of the shoulders. Some rugs have a sheepskin pad sewn on where they lie on the withers, to prevent rubbing; if yours hasn't, it is a good idea to sew one in yourself.

If using a blanket underneath the rug, this of course must be put on first. As a safety precaution against slipping, use the method shown in the diagram.

Off-rugging
When taking the rug off, first remove the roller or surcingle, before undoing the chest strap. (When rugging up, you fastened the chest strap before buckling up the roller.) This is a precaution to prevent the rug from sliding over the hindquarters and perhaps frightening the horse by getting entangled in his hind legs.

The New Zealand rug, showing how to fit the back straps

Next, fold the front half of rug and blankets back over the rear portion, and remove them by lifting them gently over the quarters, following the lie of the horse's coat. In this way the rug is neatly folded, and can be hung over the bottom half of the stable door.

There is another point which should be mentioned with regard to safety. Some people put on the rug after exercising, fasten the roller and, if the horse is still hot, turn the front of the rug back to allow his shoulders to cool off. This can be dangerous, as, without the chest strap to prevent it, the rug is inclined to work backwards and could end up tangled round the horse's hind legs.

The New Zealand rug

I have left this until last as it is not, strictly speaking, a stable rug, and should not be used on the horse indoors. It is made of waterproof canvas, and is used to keep a clipped horse warm when turned out to grass. Unless the weather is abnormally cold, an unclipped horse should not need a rug, provided there is plenty of shelter in the field.

When putting on this rug, be very careful that the leg straps, which have metal clips at the ends, do not bang against the horse as you throw it over the back. The leg straps go around the hind legs to prevent the rug from falling sideways if the horse rolls. They should be linked to prevent the legs from being chafed.

Extra care must be taken to accustom the horse to this rug before turning him out in it. Accidents have happened because a horse has panicked at feeling the strange straps around his legs and hearing the creaking of the canvas. If your horse is turned out for any length of time in a New Zealand rug, it must be carefully inspected every day. The straps soon become hard and mud-caked if not frequently oiled, and rubs and sores will result.

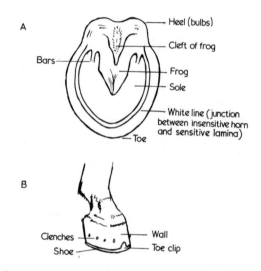

(A) the parts of the foot; (B) a neatly shod foot

Shoeing

Care of the horse's feet is one of the most important aspects of stable management, and, from the safety point of view, absolutely essential. If shoes are nailed on carelessly, they can not only lame the horse, but could cause an accident. For example, if the heel of the shoe is too long and protrudes beyond the foot, the horse is liable to step on it with the toe of the hind shoe, and will be brought down. Great care should be taken to ensure that your horse is correctly shod and his feet kept in good condition. Try to learn as much as possible about the actual structure of a horse's foot – in this way you will be able to appreciate the skill that is required by the farrier to nail on a shoe without harming the horse.

On average, horses require shoeing about once a month. If they are hunting or doing a lot of road work, it could be more often; conversely, if they spend a lot of time in the field, the shoes could last much longer. Horses at grass, if unshod, must have their feet trimmed periodically, otherwise they will grow too long and begin to crack. When the foot is too long, the edges of the hoof begin to curl outwards, and in extreme cases the horse will begin to walk on his heels. I have seen donkeys with feet that have grown so long that they have actually begun to turn upwards. This is extreme cruelty, the result of either ignorance or laziness.

A horse needs re-shoeing if :

1 The shoe has worn thin. When it has worn down to approximately one-third of its original thickness, it is time the horse was shod.
2 The shoe is loose.
3 The clenches (the ends of the nails that lie flat on the wall of the hoof) have risen.
4 The foot has grown over the edge of the shoe.
5 The foot has grown too long and therefore out of shape.
6 The shoe has been 'cast' (come off).

When you take your horse to the farrier, you can be of great assistance to him by concentrating on what is going on. Ensure that the horse is standing squarely, and that his legs can be picked up in turn without him overbalancing. Don't let him nibble at the farrier's clothes or wander about. It can be very annoying to a busy blacksmith if your horse is undisciplined or will not pick his feet up when asked. Never be afraid to ask questions – the more you can learn about your horse's feet, the safer both you and he will be.

It is most important to prepare a young horse carefully before taking him to the blacksmith for the first time. Get him accustomed to having his feet picked up and gently banged with a hammer. Teach him to bring each leg forward and up, in addition to picking them up in the normal way, as the farrier will need them in this position in order to rasp the clenches. It is most unfair to any farrier to expect him to spend time and trouble trying to shoe a nervous young horse who has never had his feet handled or been taught how to balance on three legs while the fourth is being held in an unaccustomed position.

The question has been asked, 'Can you ride an unshod horse?' The answer is, 'It depends.' Young horses that have never been shod usually have sound, hard feet, and if they are trimmed regularly the horse can be ridden for some time without shoes, provided there is very little road work, and none at all on rough gravel surfaces. Obviously, the feet would not stand up to a day's hunting. However, once the horse has been shod the feet lose a certain amount of hardness, and he will then need shoeing regularly.

When your horse has been shod, check the following:

1 That the shoe fits snugly all round and that there is no iron protruding beyond the foot.

2 That the clenches are evenly placed around the wall of the hoof, ie in line. A nail which is driven in so that the end comes out too high up the wall could be too close to the sensitive structures, or have pierced them ('pricked foot'), and the horse will go lame.

3 That the frog is in contact with the ground. This can be checked by placing a flat piece of wood, a ruler perhaps, across the bearing surface of the shoe; the frog should come into contact with it. The frog is of vital importance to the health of the foot, and acts as an anti-concussion device. Its powers as a shock-absorber will be diminished if it is not allowed to touch the ground.

4 That the foot is not too long. If the foot has not been reduced in length, the wall will have grown so that the frog is unable to reach the ground, and also the horse's weight will be forced on to the heels.

5 That the weight of the shoe is not too heavy for the type of horse. The farrier himself is the only person who can advise

you on this. Horses' feet vary considerably in structure, and some are able to carry a heavier shoe than others. It depends also on the type of work the horse is expected to do. For example, heavy shoes would be unsuitable for showing, as they would affect his way of going. This, of course, would also apply to racing.

Care of teeth

The care of a horse's teeth may seem to have little to do with safety, but in fact it plays a significant part. If his teeth are causing him pain or discomfort, it will affect his behaviour : he may start tossing his head, refuse to go forward, or rear. It is surprising how few people ever bother to look inside a horse's mouth, and will accuse the horse of bad behaviour instead of blaming themselves for their own neglect.

Horses often develop sharp edges on the molars (the grinding teeth at the back) which cut into the tongue or cheeks. This will prevent them from chewing their food properly, and if very painful may stop them from eating altogether. Ask your vet to check the teeth and rasp off any sharp edges. You can check them yourself by holding the horse's tongue out to one side of the mouth so that he cannot bite your fingers and feeling the edges of the teeth with your free hand.

Another cause of trouble on occasions are 'wolf teeth' which appear in the upper jaw just in front of the molars. They are not always present, but sometimes cause trouble by interfering with the bit and becoming sore. The vet will advise as to whether they need to be taken out.

Up to the age of five, the horse replaces temporary teeth with permanent ones each year, but at five years old he has a 'full mouth' of permanent teeth. It is well known, of course, that the age of a horse can be judged by the teeth, but only up to ten years; after that age, it is difficult to tell with any accuracy.

7

Safety at Grass

Horses and ponies are turned out to grass for various reasons. Those whose work is seasonal, such as hunters, eventers and polo ponies, are turned out for a rest and a change of diet. Others whose work is not so demanding – brood mares, ponies, riding school horses etc – can sometimes be kept at grass all the year round, provided they are adequately fed during the winter months.

If your horse is kept at grass his safety will depend entirely on your vigilance and good management. Before you turn him out you should ask yourself the following questions:

1 Is the area large enough to allow adequate grazing?
2 Is it fairly level?
3 Is the fencing sound?
4 Are there any sharp projections anywhere on which the horse could injure himself?
5 Is there adequate shelter?
6 Is water available at all times?
7 Are there any poisonous weeds in the field?

Size of field and pasture management

Keeping a horse in a restricted area requires constant diligence if you are to avoid over-grazing and a worm-infested paddock.

To prevent over-grazing it is essential that the area is large enough for it to be grazed in rotation, allowing one part to be rested and treated as required while the horse grazes on the other. It is of course impossible to give exact dimensions, as these depend on the size and type of horse and the fertility of the soil, but as a general guide, one horse would need at least 2 acres (0.8 hectares). If there is only one field, rotational grazing can be accomplished by erecting a fence across the middle so that one half can be manured or sprayed as required while the horse grazes the other half. Land which is never rested or fertilised will soon become 'horse-sick' and a breeding-ground for a multitude of worms to which horses are prone.

Before you put a fertiliser on the field, it is an excellent idea to have the soil analysed so that you can be assured of using the correct mixture which will be of benefit to your particular land. This can be done by contacting your local office of ADAS (Agricultural Development and Advisory Service), who for a small fee will come and take a sample. Alternatively, tests can be made by certain suppliers of fertilisers, who may do it free of charge.

Remember that after fertiliser has been applied, usually in the early spring, the horse must be kept off the pasture until the rain has washed all traces of it into the soil. It will not be safe to return him to the field for at least three weeks. If possible a good harrowing would aerate the soil and allow the manure to sink in and be absorbed, but this of course may not be practical, unless you know a farmer who would be willing to do it for you.

Unfortunately, horses are notoriously bad grazers, in that they will only eat certain portions of the pasture, leaving the rest to grow rank and long. If it is possible to turn cattle on to the field for a short period, they will be of great benefit, both by eating the rank grass and by swallowing the worm larvae, which will not survive in the intestines of cattle. Sheep also are useful scavengers, but they are not so easy to keep penned in the field.

Very hilly fields are not suitable for horses, particularly young ones, as they impose an extra strain on the limbs.

Fencing

Sound, safe fencing is essential in any paddock. Any fencing that is thrown together as a makeshift, such as old iron railings, bedsteads, thorn bushes etc, is dangerous. Many accidents are caused by straying animals that have managed to push through inadequate fences, and it would be prudent to check with your

The dangers of a makeshift fence

insurance agent to find out whether you are insured for damage incurred by a straying horse.

Post-and-rail fencing is generally considered to be the safest, but it is expensive to erect and does not give shelter.

Plain wire of the heavy-gauge type is adequate, as long as it is stretched tight and the bottom strand is at least 2ft (60cm) above the ground so that a pawing horse could not get a foot caught in it. Strong, solid straining posts are necessary to keep the wire taut, and some bits of cloth or tough ribbon should be tied at intervals along the top strand to attract the horse's attention, as he may not find it easy to see when galloping about. Alternatively, have the top rail made of timber to make him aware of a barrier.

Barbed wire, for obvious reasons, should never be used anywhere in the field, not even as a stop-gap. Some of the lacerations it can inflict are horrific.

Electric fencing is sometimes used, but that too can be dangerous, as it is difficult to see and is inclined to make horses nervous, particularly hunters, who are apt to panic if caught up in wire when out hunting.

The ideal type of fence is a solid, thick *hedge,* which affords both shelter and a safe enclosure.

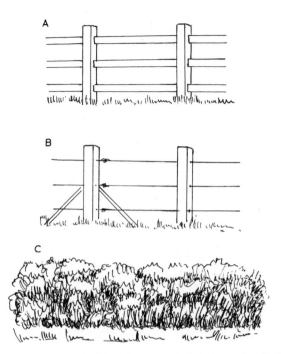

Types of enclosure suited to horses : (A) post-and-rail fencing; (B) plain wire; (C) solid hedge

Worms

It is a sad fact that many people either never bother to worm their horses at all or think that twice a year will be sufficient. If only these people could look inside a horse whose stomach and intestines have been eaten away by hordes of worms, they would perhaps be more careful. The diagram on p. 92 shows how many different species there are and where they attack. All horses harbour a certain number of worms, but with judicious dosing they will do no harm. Horses and ponies kept on a restricted area must be dosed every two months if these damaging parasites are to be kept under control. There are a number of anthelmintics which have been produced to combat the different types of worms, and it is advisable to change from one to another from time to time so that the worms do not set up an immunity

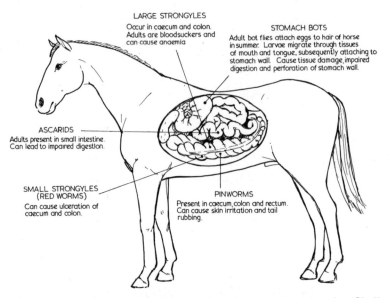

LARGE STRONGYLES
Occur in caecum and colon.
Adults are bloodsuckers and
can cause anaemia

STOMACH BOTS
Adult bot flies attach eggs to hair of horse
in summer. Larvae migrate through tissues
of mouth and tongue, subsequently attaching to
stomach wall. Cause tissue damage, impaired
digestion and perforation of stomach wall.

ASCARIDS
Adults present in small intestine.
Can lead to impaired digestion.

SMALL STRONGYLES
(RED WORMS)
Can cause ulceration of
caecum and colon.

PINWORMS
Present in caecum, colon and rectum.
Can cause skin irritation and tail
rubbing.

Occurrence of worms in horses (based on a drawing by Shell
International Chemical Co Ltd)

to one particular kind. In order to ascertain the level of infesta-
tion in your horse, take a sample of the droppings to the vet,
who will have them analysed and advise the appropriate wormer.

To keep the field as worm-free as possible, it is essential that
the droppings are picked up as often as you can manage. Ideally
this should be done every day so that the larvae have no chance
of hatching and infecting the grass. If the droppings are allowed
to remain, a lot of good grazing can also be lost, as they kill the
grass underneath.

Other hazards

Before turning a horse out, always inspect the field to make sure
that there is no debris lying around. Never leave string or wire
from hay bales anywhere within reach. Remove all plastic
manure bags. If your field is near a road, keep an eye on trippers,
who are apt to stop for a picnic and then throw their rubbish
over the hedge.

Ensure that there are no deep ditches or drains in the field:

these are especially dangerous for young foals, who may fall into them and be unable to get out.

Shelter

It is essential for the comfort and well-being of your horse that he is provided with some form of shelter. A thick hedge or trees will protect him from the weather in winter, but if the field has neither, a simple shed should be erected. It need not be elaborate, but must have a wide entrance, and plenty of room, especially if needed to accommodate more than one horse. A three-sided building, open in the front, is adequate as long as it gives shelter from the prevailing winds. This will also provide protection against flies in the summer.

Water

Clean, fresh water must be available at all times. If there is no natural supply such as a running stream or pond, a self-filling trough is ideal, but make sure that the ball-cock is enclosed so that the horse cannot interfere with it. If a pond supplies the water, it must not be stagnant or have sewage draining into it. Check all sources of supply frequently in frosty weather in case of icing.

If containers other than troughs are used, make sure that they cannot be tipped over, and that they have no sharp edges on which the horse could injure himself. Some people use old baths, but these have sharp rims and may injure a horse's knee if he lifts it suddenly while pawing. A horse will drink up to ten gallons per day in hot weather, so ensure that the container is big enough. All receptacles must be thoroughly scrubbed out at regular intervals, as they tend to become slimy and encrusted with grime.

Poisonous plants

It is very important to inspect both field and hedges carefully to ensure that there are no poisonous weeds. If you are not sure that you would recognise them, pick samples and take them to an expert to identify. Ragwort, which has yellow flowers and ragged-edged leaves, is among the most deadly, and can cause death within a few days. It is even more poisonous in its dying stages, and must not be left in the field, particularly if cut with the hay. All plants must be uprooted and burnt. Yew is also deadly, causing death in a very short time. Laurel, privet, laburnum, deadly nightshade, hemlock, horsetails, wild arum, foxglove, acorns (and green oak leaves in the spring), ground ivy and some kinds of vetch are all poisonous and must be eradicated for safety. Some plants are dangerous only when eaten in excess – bracken and buttercups come into this category – and heavily infested fields should be sprayed. Dead buttercups eaten with the hay are harmless. Mouldy hay can also be dangerous owing to toxins produced by the mould fungi.

The symptoms of poisoning in a horse are staggering, loss of appetite, lethargy, and sometimes scouring or constipation. The vet must be called immediately if you suspect poison.

Daily attention

It is important that horses at grass should be seen *every day*. This may seem unnecessary, but anyone who has looked after horses for any length of time will agree that it is always on the very day that you neglect to see him that your horse will either step on a nail, cast a shoe, try to jump out, get a foot caught up somewhere, cut himself, or get kicked by another horse! It is amazing how some horses will find trouble even in a 'safe' field.

Get into the habit of looking for cuts or scratches every time you go into the field, and at the same time check the horse's feet for cracks or rough edges, if not shod, or to see whether he needs shoeing again, if already shod.

Inspect the horse carefully during wet weather; some horses can suffer from a condition known as 'rain scald'. This is caused by the dermatophilus fungus which thrives in wet conditions. The hair along the back and on top of the hindquarters becomes matted, and pus forms under the skin. If this happens consult your vet.

Wet, muddy fields can also cause 'cracked heels' which correspond to chapped hands in human beings, and is an inflammation of the skin on the heels and legs. Again your vet will advise on treatment, but to help prevent it from occurring rub the heels and behind the pasterns with vaseline.

Catching the horse

If a horse is difficult to catch, there is usually a very good reason for it. Either he associates being caught with something unpleasant, for example rough handling or work which he does not enjoy, or he is suspicious of the person trying to catch him. The first essential, therefore, is to gain his confidence. A little bribery from the feed tin will almost always achieve this. Encourage him to come to the gate at your call; if you have the patience to wait quietly, most horses will walk up to you for a feed or a titbit. If at first he is difficult to catch, never chase him or lose your temper – this will only guarantee failure. While he is eating, slip the lead rope of the headcollar around his neck; once caught he will then submit to having the headcollar put on. If a horse is at all nervous of being caught, it is safer to use a headcollar and not a halter, as the latter has to be pushed up over the ears, whereas the headcollar strap can be placed behind them without touching them (see the diagrams on pp. 22 and 23). Never try to catch him with a bridle, for the same reason; in addition, the head must be brushed clean of any dried mud before the bridle can be comfortably fitted.

In the interests of safety, never ride a horse wearing only a headcollar, particularly if you have to ride on a road. However quiet the horse may be, if he is suddenly startled you will have no control.

If the horse is turned out with several others, it is safer to walk up to him rather than make him come to you. If you call him to the gate, the others are likely to come galloping at the same time, and the result may be a kicking match.

Turning out

When turning a horse loose into the field, always turn him round to face the gate before releasing him. Some horses will swing round and buck and kick as soon as they are free, and by turning his head towards the gate you will be in a better position to keep out of his way. Never allow the horse to get into the habit of rushing off as soon as he is released; make him stand quietly so that you have plenty of time to unfasten the head-collar. You can achieve this by occasionally giving him a titbit after removing the headcollar.

It is always safer to remove headcollars from horses at grass, as they could get a foot caught in them when scratching, or hook them on the branch of a tree or the latch of a gate.

If you are putting a horse into a strange field for the first time, do so after he has been exercised, when he is more likely to be tired and hungry. He will settle down to eat, instead of galloping around as some horses are apt to do in an unfamiliar field.

Extra feeding

A horse that is out at grass all the year round will need supplementary feeding when the herbage loses its nutritional value, which will be from about August until the following April, depending of course on the quality of grass available. During cold weather the horse uses food to keep himself warm, and in these circumstances he will, of course, need extra.

It is almost impossible to give exact quantities of food, as it could be misleading. The amount you would give to a horse doing no work at all, for example, would differ considerably from that given to one using up a lot of energy. The horse's condition will soon tell you if he is receiving the right amount: it will deteriorate if he is not being given enough, whereas if he is becoming fat and bumptious, he is having too much. To give you a very rough idea, however, an average riding horse, perhaps only ridden at weekends, would need a full haynet twice a day (12–16lb, or 5.4–7.3kg), and about 6–8lb (2.7–3.6kg) of dry food divided into two feeds, morning and evening. This might consist of oats, bran, flaked maize or cubes, or a mixture (see chapter 6). Other additives can of course be given, and remember that the horse needs a certain amount of salt. Ask your feed merchant about outdoor salt licks.

The haynet can be hung up in any convenient *sheltered* spot, or in the shed if one is provided. If the ground is wet and becomes poached where the horse is standing, move the net to another sheltered part of the field. Make sure the feed container cannot be knocked over. Various heavy-duty containers can be bought at saddle shops, but a cheap substitute is shown below. The bucket stands in the middle of two old car tyres fastened together.

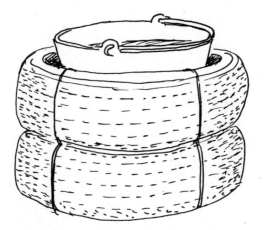

A simple, cheap feed container that cannot be tipped over

Summer grass

When turning a horse into lush grass, allow him only a short grazing period initially. Half an hour will be sufficient if it is very rich, otherwise he may get colic.

Ponies are very susceptible to 'laminitis' (fever of the feet) if allowed to become too fat on rich grass, and should be strictly rationed if showing signs of rotundity.

During the summer months, no extra feed is needed unless the horse is doing a lot of work, or unless it is a very dry summer and the grass dries up.

Grooming

Horses at grass do not need much grooming, except to make them comfortable and respectable before being ridden. The natural oil and grease should be left in the coat to give protection against cold and rain.

8

Talking of Tack

It is not an exaggeration to say that your life could depend on the condition of your tack (saddlery). A broken rein or girth at the crucial moment could cause a fatal accident. Hard, dirt-encrusted leather will crack easily and it not only dangerous but also uncomfortable for the horse.

Get into the habit of examining your saddle, bridle etc frequently. Check all stitching, worn parts (particularly where the buckles of the stirrup leathers rest, as this part wears quickly), girth straps, buckles, and the joints of bits, which over a period of time wear thin and become unable to stand any strain. Old rubber snaffles can be dangerous, as, if not checked occasionally, the chain which runs through the rubber can rust, and this could remain undetected until it snapped in half. Reins which are stitched on to the bit instead of being attached by a buckle or stud should be inspected carefully, as saliva from the horse's mouth is inclined to rot the stitching.

If possible always buy the best-quality leather; it is safer, and will last longer than cheap saddlery. Be wary of buying at sales, unless the equipment is guaranteed. A saddle may look smart, but the 'tree' (the framework on which it is built) could be broken or damaged. Stainless steel bits and stirrup irons cost more than nickel, but are supposed to be stronger and will last longer.

The dropped noseband

There is a vast variety of bits, reins, nosebands, martingales, and gadgets for varying purposes, but these should only be used by those who understand them and are able to appreciate their value. It is foolhardy to put some complicated piece of tack on your horse merely because 'Harvey Smith uses one' or 'I saw it on David Broome's horse'.

A lot of unnecessary discomfort is caused to horses by inexperienced riders using items of tack which they do not understand and cannot fit correctly. These are far too numerous to mention them all, but one item seems to have become 'the fashion', and it is so often incorrectly fitted, and abused, that I think it ought to be pointed out. This is the 'dropped noseband'. Its use has become very widespread, and I am convinced that half the horses who wear them do not need them. Its purpose is to improve control by preventing the horse from opening his mouth. It should be fitted so that the front part of the strap is well above the nostrils and not interfering with the horse's breathing, while the back part, which goes below the bit and in the chin groove, should be just loose enough to allow the horse to move his jaws freely, but not to open his mouth. In the hands of an experienced rider, it can be an asset to training, but I have seen many, put on incorrectly, which are actually harmful to the horse, being so low down on the nose that they restrict his breathing, and so tight that his jaws are clamped together and he is unable to move them at all. Some riders are not even sure why they use a dropped noseband; one person, on being asked, replied, 'I don't know, but so and so told me to use it'!

The dropped noseband

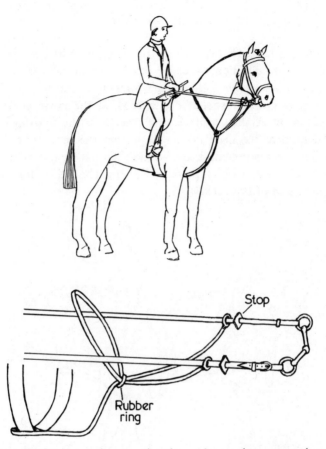

Stop

Rubber
ring

A correctly fitted running martingale, and an enlargement showing the correct fitting of the 'stops'

Martingales

Martingales too are used to give the rider extra control. There are several varieties, but the most commonly used are the running martingale and the standing martingale. Both must be fitted correctly if they are to be safe and effective.

The running martingale is a piece of leather which is attached at one end, through the horse's forelegs, to the girth, while the other end divides into two straps, each with a ring at the extremity through which the reins pass. It is supported by a neck strap. It is intended to give the rider more control if the horse attempts to raise his head above the angle required for correct balance and collection. A badly fitted martingale, with a loop hanging down between the horse's forelegs, is not only too long to be effective, but could be dangerous if the horse got a leg caught in it. A thick rubber ring placed on the martingale at the bottom of the neck strap will prevent this loop from forming. The neck strap must not be too tight: it should admit the width of a hand at the top of the withers. The buckle fastens on the near side of the neck.

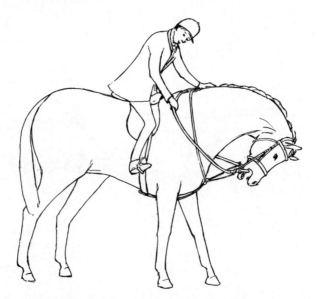

The rings of the martingale caught on the buckles of the reins: the horse cannot balance himself and may be brought down

When using a running martingale, always ensure that 'stops' are placed on the reins to prevent the rings of the martingale from getting caught on the buckles of the reins. If this should happen, particularly when jumping, it could be extremely dangerous, as the horse would be unable to use his head and neck to balance himself, and could be brought down.

If you are riding a young, excitable horse who is inclined to throw his head up and down or play with the reins, it is safer to have the branched straps of the martingale blocked in with a piece of leather. This is called a 'bib martingale', and prevents the horse from getting his teeth caught in one of the branches. I have seen several young horses in a blind panic when this has happened : they have either reared, whipped round in a circle, or run backwards out of control.

The standing martingale is attached to the girth in a similar manner to the running martingale, but the other end is fixed to the cavesson noseband (the ordinary noseband which is part of a

The bib martingale

complete bridle). Never attach it to a dropped noseband, as it would be much too severe. It should be fitted so that it only comes into effect if the horse raises his head higher than is desirable for correct balance or collection. If it is too short it will drag the horse's head down, and if too long, will be ineffective.

Balance

A horse without a rider balances himself to suit his own purposes, by using his head and neck as a balancing pole. For example, when galloping, he lowers and stretches his head and neck, and his weight naturally falls on to his front legs. The rider, in order to make the horse 'light in hand', ie to control him with the lightest of touches on the reins, needs to shift that weight further towards the back, teaching the horse to take more weight on the hind legs and not to lean on the reins. To do this the horse's hind legs must be brought forward more deeply underneath the body. This is a very simple explanation of the term 'balance', but it takes a lot of time and training to achieve.

Collection

This can only be achieved after the horse is balanced. It means collecting the whole of his body into a shortened form, with the hind legs taking even more of the weight, so that the horse is in a position to obey instantly the lightest touch of the rider's hand and leg. For example, it would enable a horse to go straight from the halt into a balanced and collected canter in one stride. Of course, the horse's centre of balance is constantly changing, according to his pace or the particular activity in which he is engaged.

These very simple explanations are merely given so that you can understand the reasons why riders often resort to martingales and other items of tack to assist them in the training of their horses.

Bits

The bit, as everyone knows, is the part of the bridle which goes into the horse's mouth, and is one of the means by which the horse is guided and controlled. There is, however, a vast number of shapes, sizes and designs, and it is important that the novice rider uses only those that can do the least damage to the horse's mouth.

Bits can be divided roughly into three categories, the snaffle, the curb and the pelham. The snaffle is generally accepted as the mildest form of bit, and can be either in one piece or jointed in the middle. The one-piece type is the gentlest, not having the nutcracker effect of the jointed one, and will do the least damage to the horse's mouth in the hands of a heavy-handed rider. Snaffles can be made of metal, rubber, vulcanite or nylon.

The curb is the harshest of all the bits, and should never be used by a beginner. Its severe action is due to the leverage obtained on the horse's mouth by the use of cheeks and a curb chain which lies in the chin groove and acts as a fulcrum. There is a variety of different designs.

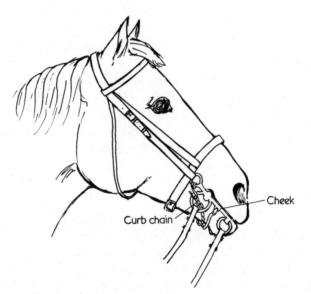

Cheek

Curb chain

The pelham bit; note the correct fitting of the curb chain to prevent the chin groove from being rubbed

The pelham is a combination of snaffle and curb. It has one mouthpiece only, but the cheeks have two rings and a curb chain attached. The top ring is for the snaffle rein, and has no leverage effect. The lower ring is for the curb rein: when this rein is used, the curb chain comes into play, acting as a lever on the mouth. The bit can be mild or severe, according to which rein is pulled.

The curb bit can also be combined with the snaffle and used as a 'double bridle', the two bits acting independently of each other. In this case, the snaffle is a much lighter, thinner bit than the normal snaffle, and is known as the 'bridoon'.

The numnah

A numnah is a shaped pad, made of sheepskin, nylon, felt or rubber, which is placed underneath the saddle. Its function is to protect the horse's back; it should not normally be necessary if the saddle is well-stuffed and correctly fitted, but sometimes a cold-backed horse will go better if wearing one, as the material used is softer and warmer for his back than the cold leather lining of most saddles. (Cold-backed horses have been discussed on pp. 23–4.)

When fitting a numnah, make sure that it is slightly larger than the saddle, otherwise the edge will be pressed into the horse's back. Before tightening the girth, the front of the numnah must be pulled up into the pommel or front arch of the saddle so that there is no pressure on the withers.

Knee caps

These are used to protect the horse's knees when travelling, or while exercising on the roads, in case he should fall and cut his knees (an accident known as 'broken knees'). The upper strap is fastened firmly on the outside of the leg, but the lower one must be loose enough to allow complete flexion of the knee.

Cleaning tack

Ideally, tack should be cleaned after every ride, but if this is not possible, do dip the bit in water to wash off any residue of saliva, particularly if the same bridle is to be used on another horse, and dry the leatherwork carefully. If this precaution is not taken, coughs and colds can be transmitted from one animal to another.

The materials needed for tack cleaning are:

Bucket of lukewarm water
Sponge for washing off dirt
Sponge for saddle soap
Tin or bar of saddle soap
Metal polish
Cleaning and polishing rags
Cloth for drying metal
Neatsfoot oil

From the safety point of view, cleaning tack is one of the most important of the stable chores. If done conscientiously, it gives an opportunity to inspect the most inaccessible parts of your saddlery. You will need a saddle horse (a wooden construction shaped so that the saddle does not rest on the gullet – the channel between the two halves of the saddle that prevents it from resting on the horse's spine). If you use a narrow bar, the saddle will rock as you clean it, which may well injure the gullet. You will also need a hook on which to hang the bridle. Both these can be bought at any saddler's, but with a bit of ingenuity you can make a saddle rest for yourself; ask an experienced person to advise you.

If there is time, both bridle and saddle should be dismantled at each cleaning session. If this is not possible, try to do it at least once a week. An occasional application of neatsfoot oil instead of soap will help to replace the natural oil of the leather. Never put oil on the outside of the saddle, as it will stain your clothes.

To clean all leatherwork, first wash off the dirt and dried sweat with a sponge dipped in warm (not hot) water. Be careful not to have the sponge too wet; saturated stitching will rot more quickly. Wipe dry with a cloth, or a chamois leather if preferred.

Next, apply saddle soap with a damp (not wet) sponge, and rub well in to the leather. If you are using the bar soap, dip the bar rather than the sponge into the water. By doing this you will ensure that the sponge is not too wet. If it is, you will find that a lather is produced which will accumulate in the buckle holes; this can be removed with a matchstick.

Pay particular attention to all the parts that are difficult to reach, such as the areas high up underneath the saddle flap, inside a folded girth, and around all buckles, studs etc. When cleaning stirrup leathers, make sure that plenty of soap is rubbed into the part where the irons hang, as it is here that the leather is most liable to crack.

Never dry leather near an open fire, as it will dry out and crack.

An excellent way of keeping folded leather girths soft and pliable is to insert a flannel strip, soaked in neatsfoot oil, between the folds. It is a good idea to change sides with your stirrup leathers each time you clean them. The nearside leather, which is used for mounting, has to withstand more pressure than the one on the off side, and may become slightly stretched; if changed over regularly they will get equal wear. You can also have them shortened occasionally from the buckle end in order to bring fresh holes into wear.

Most girths have two buckles at each end for safety, but the ones made of webbing usually have only one. Webbing girths are not entirely reliable, so if you decide to use them, always wear two for extra security.

Wash and thoroughly dry bits and stirrup irons, and then use metal polish in the normal way. When cleaning the bit, avoid getting polish on the mouthpiece, as the taste will be unpleasant for the horse.

Storing of tack

If tack is going to be stored for any length of time, cover all the leather parts with a coating of vaseline. This will preserve the leather, as it does not dry out or decompose when exposed to air. Keep the dust off either by packing everything away in an old trunk or by covering it with sheets.

If you have to put a saddle on the ground, place it on the pommel, with the girth folded underneath to protect it from being scratched. If it is thrown down carelessly, you may damage the tree.

Special shaped hangings and brackets are available in the saddler's to hang up bridles and saddles, shaped to suit them. If you hang a bridle on a nail, for example, it will be liable to cut into the leather; an old saddle-soap tin nailed to the wall makes an excellent and cheap substitute for a bridle hanger.

9

First Aid for
the Horse

Accidents will occasionally happen, even in the best of establishments. Every rider or horse owner should know something of first aid, as applied both to the horse and to the rider.

Veterinary care, however, is such a vast subject that this chapter is only intended to point out some of the things that can be done to alleviate suffering, prevent further damage and keep the animal safe until professional help is available. Unless you have had special training, or are very experienced, it is always dangerous to take too much upon yourself in the treatment of any illness or injury to the horse. The administration of 'first aid' should not present the animal with an additional hazard!

There is always a risk in listening to other people's accounts of how they cured their horse and what treatment they gave him; although the symptoms may have sounded the same, the actual illness could have been entirely different from that of your own horse, and the 'cure' could do more harm than good. Ask the advice of your vet in the first instance; it is unfair to use him as a last resort when all your 'cures' have failed.

Always be prepared for an emergency by having two well-stocked first-aid boxes, one for the horse and another for the rider, and ensure that everyone in the stable knows where to find them.

Suggested contents for the horse's first-aid box

Thermometer
Surgical scissors (blunt)
Gamgee (cotton wool with a tissue covering)
Packets of lint

Cotton wool
Wool and crêpe bandages
Surgical spirit
Sterile gauze and pads
Disinfectant (for stables)
Antibiotic dusting powder
Oiled silk or mackintosh (for use when poulticing)
Lead lotion (for cooling)
Kaolin paste
Common salt
Epsom salts

Keep all medicines, dressings etc in a dry, clean cabinet. Everything should be clearly labelled with the date on which it was acquired. Medicine that has become stale should be carefully disposed of in a safe place. Never throw bottles, plastic containers, cartons etc on the muck heap; when the manure is spread on the fields, they could be very dangerous to other animals. Never put medicine of any kind in an unmarked bottle, and check with your vet to ensure that your treatment is the correct one before administering it.

The danger of keeping any liquid in an unmarked container is illustrated by the following incident which happened on a Cornish farm. One of the cows didn't seem too well, so the farmer decided to give her a drench. He found an unlabelled bottle filled with what he thought was a cow drench, and gave the animal the whole bottleful, only to discover some time later, to his horror, that the bottle had contained liquid detergent. Luckily, the animal survived; in fact for several days afterwards it was literally 'bubbling over'!

Treatment of wounds

If the wound is severe, your first priority is to stop the bleeding. An artery that has been severed will produce bright red blood that is pumped out in spurts, and the bleeding must be stopped as soon as possible. Apply a sterile pad of gauze and bandage

very firmly around the affected area, keeping the pressure evenly
distributed, both above and below the wound. If a bandage is
unavailable, use a clean cloth, towel, or even your shirt in an
emergency, and press it directly on to the wound itself. Do not
use a tourniquet: unless it is expertly applied it can do more
harm than good. If the wound is in a place where it is not
possible to bandage, such as the head or abdomen, apply direct
pressure as described above. With a wound of any severity it is
always safest to call the vet, who will advise on further treatment.

If the wound is slight, allow the bleeding to stop of its own
accord. Clean it thoroughly, either with a *mild* antiseptic or a
little salt and water, or, preferably, by allowing clean water from
the hosepipe to trickle gently over it for at least ten minutes. It
is a great mistake to think that by bathing with a strong antiseptic you will encourage healing; in fact you will delay it. Do
not use a sponge, as it will be liable to contain germs.

Finally, dust with an antibiotic powder. It is not necessary
to bandage small wounds: they will probably heal more quickly
if the air is allowed to get at them, but they must be kept
scrupulously clean. Do not be in too much of a hurry for a wound
to heal; the essential thing is to keep it clean, and give it time
to heal from the base towards the outside.

Puncture wounds

This type of wound is usually caused by a nail, thorn, piece of
glass or a sharp flint. Occasionally, a farrier accidentally drives
a nail into the sensitive part of the foot. As there is very little
blood as a rule, the wound can go unnoticed although the
penetration may have been deep; this makes it particularly
dangerous. To add to the hazards, there is a grave risk of tetanus
(lockjaw), as the wound heals over rapidly and excludes air, a
condition in which the tetanus germ thrives. As a result of this
initial surface healing, pus can be enclosed inside the wound, in
which case it should be poulticed (see p. 114).

Tetanus

All horses should be immunised against this terrible disease *before* an accident occurs. In nine cases out of ten, by the time the symptoms become apparent it is too late to prevent death. To watch a horse slowly dying of tetanus is a harrowing experience, and one which can easily be avoided.

It is commonly supposed that a horse can be immunised for life by one tetanus injection. *This is not true.* After the initial injection, a booster has to be given four to six weeks later, followed by another after a further year. In districts where the tetanus germ is prevalent, the horse may need an annual dose of serum.

There is now, in fact, a combined injection which offers protection against both tetanus and equine 'flu.

Sprains and bruises

Most injuries caused by kicks or knocks, where the skin is not broken, will be apparent from the presence of heat or swelling. Both can be reduced by running cold water from the hose over the affected part. Always work from the hoof up to the bruise itself, and start hosing with a gentle trickle; a sudden gush of cold water will probably frighten the horse.

Sprained tendons, which occur most frequently in the forelegs, are a more serious matter. They can be caused in many ways, but the most usual are landing heavily from a fence; too much galloping, especially in boggy ground, when the horse is young; being pulled up suddenly; or faulty shoeing. Occasionally they are due to defective conformation, for example over-long pasterns, which throw extra weight on the tendons. The symptoms are pain and tenderness in the tendons at the back of the cannon bone, heat and swelling.

Treatment will depend on the severity of the sprain, but rest is always essential. Cold-water hosing may be adequate in mild cases, but in more serious ones the vet's advice must be sought.

Eye injuries

If the horse has something stuck in his eye, only remove it if you can do so easily. It would be safer to call the vet and keep the animal in a darkened place until he arrives. Someone should stay with the horse to prevent him from rubbing the eye and making the damage worse.

Saddle and girth galls

These sore patches are a sign of bad horse management, and should not be allowed to develop. Saddles that do not fit properly, or backs that are dirty, will cause friction and subsequent raw places. A horse just up from grass, or a young one in soft condition and unused to wearing a girth, will be vulnerable to girth galls and should be carefully checked.

Make sure that all your tack is clean, particularly the underpart of the saddle; if it is encrusted with dirt, it will rub the horse's back. If a leather girth is causing trouble, change to a string one, or alternatively, encase the leather one in sheepskin.

If you find that the skin is becoming tender, it can be hardened by rubbing gently with surgical spirit or a mild solution of salt and water, but if it is already raw, apply a cooling lotion. Keep the saddle off the horse until the sore places have healed.

Poulticing

Where pus is present, hot poultices will soften the tissue and allow the pus to come to the surface. They can be made in several different ways.

Kaolin paste is used in much the same way as it would be with a human being. The paste is heated up, either by standing the tin in boiling water or by spreading the cold paste between two pieces of thin gauze, placing it on an old tin plate or heatproof dish and heating it up in the oven (I find this method easier). By spreading the kaolin on gauze rather than applying it directly to the wound, you are able to remove it more easily and speedily if it proves too hot. Test the temperature on the back of your hand before applying it to the wound. Cover the poultice with lint or cotton wool, and then wrap a piece of oiled

silk or mackintosh around the dressing to keep the heat in.
Bandage fairly loosely to allow for swelling.

Foot poultices can also be made with bran. Into a bucket
put enough bran to cover the affected part, and pour on a little
boiling water. The bran should be damp, not wet, and an antiseptic should be added. Put the poultice on a piece of sacking
which is laid on the ground, then get the horse to stand on it
with the affected foot. Tie the sacking up around the fetlock and,
to prevent it from slipping down, bandage over the ends of the
sacking with a stable bandage.

Poultices ought to be changed every twelve hours, otherwise
they lose their benefit.

Epsom salts

A useful way of taking the heat out of a horse's legs is to make
a paste of Epsom salts and cold water. Apply around the cannon
bones and tendons, cover with gamgee or cotton wool, and put
on a stable bandage. Leave on all night.

How to detect lameness

Surprisingly, there are a number of people who know when a
horse is lame but cannot tell which leg is affected. If you think
about it, your own reaction to a sore foot will help you to decide
on which leg the horse is lame. If you have a stone in your shoe,
you put as little weight on that foot as possible. It is the same
with the horse. If he is lame in a foreleg, he will lessen the weight
on the affected one by raising his head each time it comes to
the ground. Similarly, if he is lame behind, the point of his hip
will be raised each time the lame leg is placed on the ground.

Unless a horse is very lame, it is easier to detect the trouble at
the trot than at the walk. It is also easier to find out on which
leg the horse is lame by having him trotted directly away from
you, so that you are able to study the movement of his hindquarters in order to detect hind-leg lameness, and then towards
you, where you have a clear view of the movement of his head,

which will indicate on which leg he is lame in front.

There are so many different causes of lameness, of course, that it is far beyond the scope of this book to deal with them all. In the majority of cases pain, heat or swelling will usually lead you to the seat of the trouble, but if they do not, it is always wise to call the vet before further damage is done.

General nursing

Always treat a sick or lame horse as gently as you would like to be treated yourself. Handle his wounds carefully, don't cause him any more suffering by being rough or unsympathetic. Make him as comfortable as you can, but with as little fuss as possible. If he is unable to lie down owing to an injured leg, keep his bedding to a minimum so that he can move more freely; otherwise, give him a deep, comfortable bed of clean, dry straw.

Avoid creating dust by shaking up the bedding, and dispense with grooming, except for a light brush over, until the horse is feeling better.

Stable bandages, with plenty of cotton wool underneath, will help the circulation in his legs and keep him warm. Never use safety pins: they could unfasten and drop into the bedding, where a horse might lie on them or even eat them. Check all bandages frequently; if a leg swells they may become too tight.

Ensure that the horse has plenty of fresh air – a warm muggy stable will not help him to recover – but avoid draughts. He must be kept warm, but not allowed to sweat. If he is not over-rugged, but is still sweating, he is probably in pain.

Clean, fresh water should be made available at all times, and the water bucket scrubbed out every day. Absolute cleanliness will minimise risk of infection.

If the horse is not well enough to be exercised, cut out all heating foods such as oats, maize, barley etc, and feed on bran mashes, grass, and plenty of good hay. Tempt his appetite with sliced carrots, apples, mangolds, any green food, and watercress, if he will eat it. Always remove any uneaten food, and keep the manger scrupulously clean.

Colic

Everyone who looks after horses should be able to recognise the symptoms of colic, which is our equivalent to a pain in the stomach. The horse will appear restless, pawing the ground and looking round at his flanks. According to the severity of the pain, he may try to roll, and will break out in a sweat. His breathing will be laboured, and the pulse faster than normal (normal rate is approximately 36–40 beats per minute). To take the pulse, feel the artery (sub-maxillary) under the lower jaw : it can be found at the angle of the jaw, on either side. Alternatively, take it at the radial artery inside the foreleg, on a level with the elbow. The normal respiration rate is 8–12 per minute – watch the rise and fall of the flanks.

The causes of colic are legion. It can be due to sudden changes of diet; giving water too soon after feeding; too much food; a stoppage; worms; fermenting food; working after a heavy meal; sand in the stomach; stones in the bowels, kidneys or bladder; or a twisted gut. Some are of the opinion that rolling causes a twist in the gut, but others say that it is the twist that causes the horse to roll in pain.

At the first signs of colic, put a headcollar on the horse and lead him around so that he cannot lie down and roll. Do not give him anything to eat or drink, and make sure that he is kept warm with blankets and rugs. The old-fashioned remedy was always to administer a colic drench, but unless this is done by an expert, the remedy can be as dangerous as the complaint. Most horses are difficult to drench, and there is a danger of getting the liquid into the lungs. If the symptoms persist after about an hour, it is safer to call the vet, who will probably give the horse an injection.

Never leave a horse on his own if he has colic; severe pain may cause him to knock himself about.

Taking the temperature

The normal temperature for a horse is 100.5°F (38°C), though of course it will vary a little according to the time of day and from horse to horse. To take the temperature, first of all make sure that the mercury is shaken down to well below the normal temperature, and apply some vaseline to the end of the thermometer. Gently lift the tail, and insert the thermometer into the rectum, standing a little to one side in case the horse kicks. Leave for the stated time, being careful to hold on to the thermometer all the while. If the reading is over 102°F (38.9°C), the horse needs professional attention.

How to recognise a sick horse

Watch your horse carefully when he is in good health, and you will soon notice the difference when he is off colour. Compare the appearance of his coat, eyes and ears, and the flare of his nostrils. (A horse in pain will breathe quickly, with wide open nostrils.) Instead of looking alert and happy, he will stand with drooping head and ears back. He will move listlessly, and show no interest. His coat may look dull and staring, and if he is feverish, he will sweat and become very thirsty. His eyes too will be dull, and the surrounding membranes inflamed.

Not all of these symptoms will appear simultaneously, of course, but always be on the lookout for anything that is out of the ordinary.

10

First Aid for
the Rider

A knowledge of first aid is very useful to anyone who works around horses, and knowing what to do in an accident could mean the difference between aggravating the injury and helping the casualty to recover more quickly.

Unfortunately, accidents often happen when you are least prepared, or when you are too far away from your first-aid box to be able to use its contents. Nevertheless, if you keep calm and think clearly, you can improvise, and use many objects that are at hand. For instance, a belt or tie could be made into a temporary bandage, or used as a sling. A shirt, torn into strips, could also be used as a bandage, or as a pad to arrest bleeding. A farm gate could be unhung and made into a stretcher.

However, if the accident happens in or near the stable, your first-aid box should provide the equipment that you need.

Suggested contents for first-aid box

Pair of scissors
Bandages of various widths
Sterile gauze
Adhesive tape
Band-Aids
Safety pins
Antiseptics (Dettol etc)
Triangular bandage or scarf for sling
Inflatable splints (only to be used by experienced first aider)

Make sure that the first-aid box is kept up to date, and place it where everyone knows where to find it.

An accident

If you think someone has been badly injured, or if he is unconscious, *do not move him,* unless of course he is in the way of some impending danger. Call a doctor immediately. While awaiting the doctor's arrival, there are four important things you must do :

1 Make sure the casualty can breathe.
2 Stop bleeding.
3 Treat for shock.
4 Immobilise any broken bones.

Breathing

If the casualty has stopped breathing, it is imperative that you give artificial respiration immediately – delay may prove fatal. Remove from the mouth any debris, mucus, false teeth, chewing gum etc that could obstruct the air passage to the lungs, and loosen clothing round the neck. Lay the patient on his back and, working from the side, tilt his head back, pulling the lower jaw forward and upwards. Pinch the nostrils tight, seal his mouth with your own and breathe deeply into his lungs. Watch for the chest to rise : if it does not, check that the tongue has not fallen back and blocked the air passage. If this happens, grasp the lower jaw, pull forwards, and tilt the head further back. The first few breaths should be given as quickly as possible, and thereafter at the rate of ten breaths per minute.

Bleeding

Severe bleeding must be checked as soon as possible, but do not panic at the sight of a little blood – it usually looks worse than it actually is. If the blood is bright red and is spurting out, an artery has been damaged, and in this case the bleeding must be stopped by applying *immediate* pressure. Place a pad of sterile gauze or, if this is not available, any clean piece of material –

shirt or handkerchief – directly over the wound, making sure it covers the whole area, and bandage very firmly. If the blood soaks through, do not remove the pad, but put another bandage on top. If the cut is only superficial and not bleeding badly, wash thoroughly with plain water or mild antiseptic, cover with a clean, dry dressing, and bandage.

Shock

In any accident, even a minor one, it is always safest to treat for shock. If the injury has been extensive, shock will always be present to some degree.

Lay the casualty down with head low and turned to one side, and raise the legs. Wrap warmly in blankets or rugs, but do not overheat by using hot water bottles. Make sure he has plenty of air but is not in a draught. Make as comfortable as possible, and loosen clothing.

DO NOT GIVE ANYTHING TO DRINK. If the patient is unconscious you will choke him, and if subsequently he has to have an anaesthetic, he must have an empty stomach.

Broken bones

Suspect a broken bone if the limb is in an unnatural position; if there is pain at the site of injury; if the injured part cannot be moved normally; or if there is swelling and discolouration. If you are not skilled in first aid, do not attempt to set a broken bone yourself, but try to prevent further damage by avoiding unnecessary movement. Keep the limb as still as possible.

Do not attempt to use splints at all unless you are very experienced.

In all cases, treat for shock.

Broken leg
Lay the patient down. Immobilise the leg by padding it and bandage both legs together, tying at knees and ankles and using plenty of padding between the legs. For padding you can use

rolled-up sweaters, pillows etc. Never try to remove the rider's boot, as you may cause further damage.

Broken collarbone
This is one of the most common of riding injuries. The rider should support the arm on the injured side with the other hand until it has been bandaged. Place a pad between the upper arm and chest and bandage the arm to the chest before supporting it with a triangular bandage or scarf. Make sure that the shoulder is kept well back, and not allowed to slump forward.

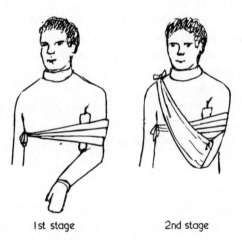

1st stage   2nd stage

How to bandage a broken collarbone

Broken arm
Treat in a similar manner to a broken collarbone. Immobilise the arm with plenty of padding between the arm and body, and place in a sling.

Back injuries
If the casualty complains of pain in the back, he should not be moved until the doctor arrives. Never try to pick him up or let him attempt to get up on his own. Keep him warm, but on no account give him anything to drink.

Head injuries
Keep the casualty lying down, but elevate the head and shoulders slightly by placing pillows underneath. Do not move him until the doctor arrives.

Broken neck
If you suspect a neck fracture, keep the casualty flat on his back and steady the head by placing a firm object on either side. *Do not lift his head* on to a pillow.

Tetanus

Tetanus germs are particularly prevalent where there are horses, and it would be wise to keep up to date with your tetanus shots. Ask your doctor to advise you.

11

Safety while Travelling

If a horse has never been in a horse box or trailer before, it is fatal to try to load him for the first time in a hurry. If he is nervous, he will sense your impatience and it will make him worse. A horse that is frightened is never safe; his reactions will be unpredictable, and panic will cloud his reason.

Some horses take no notice at all of travelling, either in a horse box or a trailer, while others need all your patience and calmness to help them overcome their anxiety. A little time spent getting your horse used to loading and unloading before you actually have to travel anywhere will pay dividends.

Preparing the horse box

It is a good idea to put some sand on the floor of the box or trailer, underneath the straw: this will give a better grip if the straw is kicked to one side. It is also important to cover the loading ramp with a thick layer of straw or matting, as some horses are frightened when they hear their feet rattling on the boards.

Hang up a net of hay for the horse to munch at, but make sure it is out of reach of pawing feet. If he is travelling with another horse, give them a net each and tie them so that they cannot bite each other. The net must be tied with a quick-release knot.

Never put horses in a box untied, as they may start fighting and injure one another.

Loading

If you are loading a young or nervous horse for the first time, try to choose a calm day; wind will make tarpaulins flap, and straw will blow around and frighten him. Never try to load him on your own, particularly into a trailer, where it is important that an assistant is on hand to fasten the tail strap or bar as soon as the horse is in to prevent him from backing out again. Ensure that the assistant does not stand directly behind the ramp, but a little to one side. If the horse suddenly rushes backwards, as he is apt to do if frightened, before the strap or bar has been fastened, the assistant may be knocked over.

Put a headcollar on the horse, not a halter : it is more secure, and less likely to twist around or be pulled over the horse's head. Attach a long lead rope so that if the horse rears the rope will not be snatched out of your hand. If you also put a bridle on top of the headcollar, it will give you extra control.

As I have already mentioned, it is a sensible idea to accustom the horse to being loaded before the actual journey, so that he is thoroughly at home in the horse box or trailer and realises that there is nothing to fear. Choose a safe place to park the trailer, away from all clutter and anything with which the horse could become entangled if he played up. Position it in a gateway or next to a hedge, so that a natural wing is provided, and if possible park so that light falls into the trailer. Horses are often nervous of going into a dark place.

Give the horse plenty of time; let him eat a mouthful of oats from a bucket, and then entice him to walk up the ramp by moving the bucket just out of his reach. If he walks in, let him finish his feed inside, and repeat this for several days until he thinks of the trailer as another stable. If the horse has confidence in you he may not need the oats to entice him, in which case lead him straight towards the ramp, walking close to his shoulder, without looking back or hesitating as you walk up the ramp.

If, in spite of your efforts, the horse refuses to load, there are several things you can do. One is to get two assistants and ask them to stand one on each side of the ramp, holding a lunge line or rope between them. As you lead the horse on to the ramp, they should simultaneously pull the rope tightly against his buttocks. This will often do the trick, but do warn them to be on the alert just in case the horse kicks.

Many unorthodox methods have been suggested to induce a stubborn horse to load, including blindfolding, driving in long reins and putting another horse in first, but the only satisfactory solution is infinite patience. Hitting the horse with a whip, or shouting at him, will only increase his fear, whereas patience and kindness will eventually eliminate it, allowing your horse to arrive at his destination cool and relaxed, instead of a sweating bundle of nerves.

The journey

The first journey that a horse experiences will either make or mar his confidence in travelling. A bad driver, who speeds around corners and jerks him off his feet when changing gear, will quickly ruin the horse's chances of becoming a good traveller, and will make him difficult to load the next time.

It is extremely tiring for a horse that is unused to travelling, to keep himself balanced, so it is important to take him on only

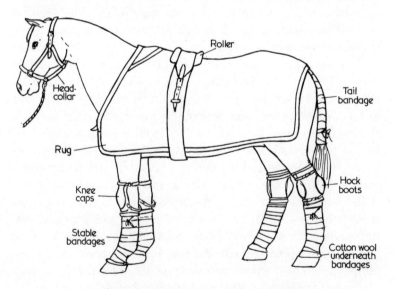

A horse correctly dressed for travelling

a short journey for the first time. If you, or someone else he is used to, could travel in the box with him, it would give him a great deal of confidence.

To protect his legs from injury, put on knee caps and stable bandages. Some horses will lean back against the tailboard and rub their tails; to prevent this, put on a tail bandage as well. If your horse is inclined to kick the sides or back of the box, you can protect his hocks with specially designed hock boots. American show horses often wear 'head bumpers', padded guards that protect the top of the head from injury. They do not seem to be used so extensively in this country, but are obviously an additional protection.

If the weather is cold or the box draughty, the horse will need a rug, but if he is nervous he will be inclined to sweat, so do not overdo the clothing.

Never leave the saddle or bridle on; either is liable to get caught up in something.

On a long journey, stop every few hours to make sure the horse is all right – and if you stop for coffee, make sure your horse is offered some water! If the weather is hot, see that there is plenty of ventilation in the trailer, and park in the shade; if it is cold and windy, try to find a sheltered spot where the wind is not blowing directly into the trailer.

Unloading

It is as important to take great care when unloading as when loading. If you hurry the horse, he is likely to get into the dangerous habit of rushing out backwards as soon as the ramp is lowered. Always make sure he is untied *before* the ramp is let down : if not he may pull back and smash his headcollar. Teach him to stand still for a few minutes after the ramp is down, and then allow him to back out quietly and calmly.

The person who is dealing with the ramp should always stand at the side, never directly behind where he could easily be knocked over if the horse rushed backwards.

Trailers that have an unloading ramp at the front, where

the horse can walk straight through and is not obliged to back out, are obviously safer.

Maintenance of trailer

Always check the floor and ramp of your box or trailer regularly to ensure that the wood has not rotted. Some terrible accidents have been caused by horses' feet going through the floorboards. Make sure that all fastenings, hitches etc are oiled and in perfect working order: you never know when you may have to get the ramp down in a hurry, and trying to unfasten a rusty catch could mean vital seconds lost.

12

Buying a Suitable
Horse

Choosing the right horse is just as big a gamble as choosing the
right husband or wife: both need a great deal of thought and
deliberation!

When buying a horse, it is important both for his sake and
your own that you should know exactly what it is going to entail.
The price you pay for the animal is only the beginning of a
long list of expenses that are sure to increase year by year. The
horse will have to be fed, housed, groomed, shod, tacked and
wormed, and will perhaps need the vet on occasions. Have you
the right facilities? Can you afford it? Do you know enough
about horse management to cope with emergencies? These are
all questions that need to be asked before you decide to buy a
horse of your own.

Far too many inexperienced people buy horses and ponies
without enough thought, and cause them untold suffering, not
intentionally, but because their knowledge is not adequate. To
quote just one example, an old man who lived on his own bought
a pony 'for a bit of company'. Knowing nothing about the care
of ponies, he tied it to an old garden roller in his back yard
with a piece of rope in which it soon became entangled. It had
to lie on concrete, had no water available, and was fed on
cornflakes! Luckily the pony was discovered in time and
rescued before too much damage was done. This type of
ignorance, however, is all too common. In fact the whole
question of horse-keeping has been brought to the notice of
certain local authorities, because so many horses and ponies are
being kept in bare, horse-sick fields.

If, after giving the matter very careful thought, you decide
that you are in a position to look after a horse, the following

may be of some assistance in giving you a rough idea of the expenses involved. It is, of course, only a very approximate estimate, based on the late 1979 prices; precise costs will depend on such factors as the size and type of horse, the area in which you live, the fluctuations of prices, the season, the state of the crops, and whether your horse is stabled or kept at grass.

A horse might cost anything from £600 upwards, a saddle from £100 upwards and a bridle from £12 upwards. The cost of a horse at livery might be £18–£20 per week, plus shoeing at £8–£14 per set.

If you look after the horse yourself and keep it stabled during the winter, the food bill alone will be considerable: hay £1–£2 per bale; oats £5–£7 per cwt (50kg); bran £7–£8 per cwt; flaked maize £8–£9 per cwt. The horse might eat approximately 10lb (4.5kg) of oats per day, and perhaps 6lb (2.7kg) of bran, plus extras (see chapter 6). You would need between 18cwt and 1 ton (900–1,000kg) of oats during a winter if your horse was hunting hard or doing any strenuous work, and about 1 ton of hay. If the horse was kept at grass, the costs would be lower if he was not ridden very much and would not require quite the same quantity of dry food, but remember that the more work he does, the more food he will need.

Assuming then that the above has not discouraged you, where do you look for a suitable mount?

Choosing the right horse

It is always safer, if possible, to buy a horse whose reputation is known to be reliable. Buying at sales is a risky business, even for the experienced, and is definitely not recommended for the novice.

Go to a person you know to be knowledgeable, perhaps a reputable dealer, riding school owner or private owner, and explain your requirements and limitations. If you are frank, and do not pretend to know more than you really do, they will feel a sense of responsibility in advising you on the type of horse best suited to your needs. State clearly the purpose for which you want the horse. Do you want to jump? Do you want it only for hacking? Do you want to show it? Perhaps you are interested in riding club activities, or hunting? The horse you intend to buy must suit you personally, so do not be too influenced by other peoples' likes and dislikes.

The most important quality to look for in your prospective purchase is temperament. A horse which 'hots up' (is easily excited), shies, is nervous in traffic or is bad-tempered, is a danger to a novice rider. Unless you want to show it, looks are unimportant, provided that it is sound. In this connection, it is always advisable to have your own vet examine any horse that you are considering buying.

Ask the vendor whether the horse has any stable vices such as crib-biting, wind-sucking or weaving (see p. 59). All these vices will detract from his value should you wish to sell him again. Do not be afraid to ask questions concerning the horse's behaviour. Is he quiet in traffic? Does he shy? Is he quiet to shoe? Is he a fussy feeder? Will he load into a trailer? Can you catch him when he is turned out to grass? Don't be like the man who bought a horse and, having paid over the cheque, said to the seller, 'Now that the horse is mine, tell me, is there anything that I ought to know about him?' The seller replied with a grin, 'Well, there are only two things wrong with him: one is, you can't catch him in the field, and the other is, he's no b—— good when you have!'

When you go to look at a prospective purchase, always ask the owner to ride it before you have a ride on it yourself. Take note of how freely it moves, and whether it seems placid or excitable. Does it leave the stable willingly or reluctantly? After the owner has shown you its paces, have a ride on it yourself. Allow the horse to walk quietly for the first few minutes so that you have time to get used to him. Never get on a strange horse and trot or canter straight away. Ask the horse to go past the entrance to the stable yard. This will tell you if he is inclined to be 'nappy' (objects to going in certain directions). Most nappy horses will pull towards their own stable. If you intend to jump him, ask the owner if you can put him over a small fence, and note whether he jumps freely or is inclined to hang back. It will not take long for you to get the feel of a horse, and to decide whether you are comfortable on him and can control him with ease.

Do not expect the seller to allow you to have the horse on trial. It is no reflection on the horse, but only natural that he would be unwilling to take the risk involved.

If you are buying a horse for the first time, you will probably want an 'all-rounder' and not a specialist in any one field. Good basic conformation, of course, is desirable in any horse, but special qualities are needed for specific activities. For example, a dressage horse should have a kind temperament, balance and free movement; a show jumper must have strength and power in his hind legs; a hunter must be sound in his wind and be able to stay; the show horse must have quality, the ability to move well, and good conformation. If you can find a horse with all these qualities you will be lucky, and it will cost you a great deal more than £600!

However, bearing in mind that you will not find a perfect horse, try to buy one that you feel happy on. If you intend to hunt, it is important to think of the type of fences that the horse will be required to jump. For example, if you live in Leicestershire, you will need a thoroughbred type of horse that can gallop and jump big fences, whereas if you live in Cornwall, where the banks and stone walls call for cleverness rather than speed, a compact, stocky type of animal would be more suitable.

Your own weight and height, of course, will also influence your choice. Make sure that you are not too heavy for your prospective purchase. The horse's height is not always an indication of how much weight he is able to carry – it depends more on his substance and amount of 'bone'. (Bone is measured around the cannon bone, just under the knee.) It is essential for an experienced person to advise you on this, but if a horse has thin spindly legs, he will be unable to carry a lot of weight.

Conformation

Having said that conformation (the form or shape of the horse) is less important than temperament for the novice buyer, there are one or two points that ought to be discussed. You should bear in mind that you may want to sell the horse eventually. As your riding improves, your demands on the horse will increase, and perhaps he will not be suitable for more advanced riding. In this event your first purchase should be 'saleable', that is, should have no obvious defects of conformation that would discourage a prospective buyer. Your vet will ensure that he is sound in wind, limb, eyes and heart, but his make and shape will be your choice. Compare the two horses in the diagrams on p. 134 and you will see the difference between a good shape and a poor one. Serious conformation faults can lead to the horse becoming unsound. For instance, if he has narrow, 'boxy' feet and upright pasterns, the resultant jarring that he will receive as he brings his feet to the ground is liable to make him go lame. Conversely, very long, sloping pasterns are equally at fault, as they will be weak and unable to carry any weight, throwing extra strain on the tendons at the back of the leg.

Without delving too deeply into details, the following are some of the points that you should check.

The head

A well-defined attractive head catches the eye. Look for pricked, alert ears and a kind expression in large, prominent eyes set well out at the side of the head. Small 'piggy' eyes are considered to be a sign of bad temper. The head should not be too large, as a heavy head interferes with the horse's natural balance.

Make sure the incisor teeth meet; a horse with a 'parrot mouth' (top jaw overlapping the bottom) cannot graze on short grass, and would need special conditions.

The neck

The neck should have a convex top line, and fit into well-developed withers and long sloping shoulders. If the shoulders are too straight, they will limit the forward movement of the front legs. A horse with a 'ewe' neck – a concave line to the top of the neck – finds it difficult to 'bridle' correctly, that is, to put

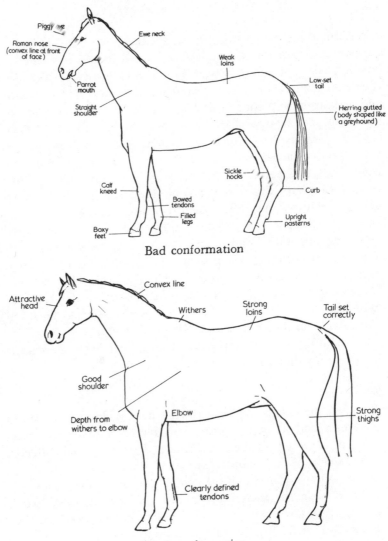

Bad conformation

- Piggy eye
- Roman nose (convex line at front of face)
- Parrot mouth
- Straight shoulder
- Ewe neck
- Weak loins
- Low-set tail
- Herring gutted (body shaped like a greyhound)
- Calf kneed
- Bowed tendons
- Filled legs
- Boxy feet
- Sickle hocks
- Curb
- Upright pasterns

Good conformation

- Attractive head
- Convex line
- Withers
- Strong loins
- Tail set correctly
- Good shoulder
- Depth from withers to elbow
- Elbow
- Strong thighs
- Clearly defined tendons

his head in a position which gives the rider maximum control.

Chest and ribs
The chest should not be too narrow, as it must allow plenty of

heart and lung room. There should be great depth from the withers to the elbow, with well-sprung ribs. Flat-sided horses often lack stamina. Also, if the chest is too narrow, the front feet will be closer together and the horse will be apt to 'brush', ie to knock one leg against the other. On the other hand, if the chest is too wide, the horse will have a rolling gait and be an uncomfortable ride.

The back and quarters
The back should be fairly short, with strong muscular loins, and the quarters round, with well-developed muscle and strong thighs. There is an old saying that 'a good horse should have a head like a duchess and a bottom like a cook'. The tail must be set high, not low down on drooping quarters. The lower part of the belly should curve upwards slightly, but should not run up between the hind legs like a greyhound.

The legs
The majority of unsoundnesses that occur in horses are to be found in legs and feet. They have to carry the whole of the horse's weight, plus that of the rider. The forelegs are the principal weight-bearers, while the hind legs are used for propulsion. It is obvious, then, that the legs and feet are the most important part of the horse's anatomy.

The legs should be 'clean', that is, should have no unwarranted lumps or bumps. The joints should be large and flat, with short cannon bones, and the tendons and ligaments clearly defined. A horse that has a tendency to swelling of the legs should be avoided.

When viewed from the front, the toes of the forelegs should point straight ahead, not inwards (a pigeon-toed horse) or outwards (a splay-footed one). The knees, viewed from the side, should give a convex appearance. If they appear concave – a condition known as 'calf knees' or 'back at the knee' – the horse should be avoided, as this is a serious weakness. A few horses appear to buckle over at the knees, which is the opposite to calf knees and is known as being 'over at the knee'. This is not quite as serious, but view the horse with suspicion, as he may be a stumbler.

The hind legs, when viewed from the side, should not appear overbent (sickle hocks), as this shape of leg predisposes to strains such as 'curbs', a thickening of the tendon or ligament at the back of the hock. When viewed from the rear, the toes of the hind legs should point straight ahead. If they turn outwards (ie the hocks appear to point towards one another) the horse is called 'cow hocked' and will be unable to move straight. Conversely, 'bowed hocks' (toes in, hocks out) are again a fault, as the horse is likely to twist the hock as the leg touches the ground, causing extra strain on it.

The feet

The horse's foot is susceptible to a variety of diseases and unsoundnesses too numerous to mention within the scope of this book. The hoof contains a complicated system of bones, tendons, sensitive laminae, insensitive laminae, sensitive sole, insensitive sole and various other components, which all have to bear not only the weight of horse and rider, but also the constant concussion of the hoof on the ground. Jorrocks, the famous sporting grocer immortalised by R. S. Surtees, sums it up when he says, 'It's not the 'unting as 'urts the 'oss, but the 'ammer, 'ammer, 'ammer on the 'ard 'igh road!'

As I have already mentioned, the feet should not be narrow in shape, but should have broad heels, with well-developed frogs and arched soles. Flat or dropped soles are prone to corns, and will be more easily bruised.

Make sure the hoofs are pairs; if one front foot, for instance, differs in shape from the other, regard it with suspicion. Also regard with suspicion the foot which appears concave and ringed, as the horse has probably suffered from 'laminitis' (inflammation of the foot) and may be prone to it.

Movement

Make sure the horse moves straight. Stand directly behind him and watch him going away from you. There should be no 'dishing' (swinging the lower part of the foreleg outwards) or 'brushing' (striking the inside leg with the opposite foot). His hind legs should follow directly in the tracks of the forelegs.

When viewed from the side, he should be seen to walk with long, sweeping strides, his hind legs being brought well forward underneath his body. At the trot, he should use his shoulders to move the forelegs forward in long, low strides; short, choppy action, with the knees elevated, usually means that he will be an uncomfortable ride.

Buying children's ponies

A few words of caution are necessary on the subject of ponies for children.

There seems to be an alarming trend nowadays for parents to buy ponies that are just not suitable for the child's standard of riding. A pony that is too strong or too lively for the child's capabilities is not only a danger to the child, but will soon destroy any confidence that he or she might have. I have been saddened at shows during the last few years to see so many incidents of sobbing, frightened children being put on ponies that they are completely incapable of controlling. This is as stupid as putting a baby on a racehorse.

Parents who have had no previous experience of buying ponies should think very carefully before buying one for their child. They have often been heard to say, 'I have bought a young pony for my three-year-old child, so that they can learn together.' This is a complete fallacy, and its dangers cannot be stressed too strongly. A novice child and a novice pony can almost be guaranteed to ruin each other's chances of success, while from the safety point of view it could be disastrous. The reactions of a young pony are unpredictable; sudden movements, loud noises, barking dogs and so on, which would leave an older pony unmoved, are much more liable to scare a young one and cause an accident to the child. Of course there are exceptions, as some young ponies, if handled correctly are as quiet as the older ones, but with the majority the risk is always there.

There are two further points concerning children's safety that I feel should be mentioned. The first is the dangerous practice of putting a child up on a horse in front of the rider. If the horse should play up, or become frightened, the child will be at risk as the rider will lose a certain amount of control.

The second is permitting a child to ride with his feet pushed through the loop of the stirrup leathers instead of in the irons. This occasionally happens when the leathers are too long and there are not enough holes to allow them to be shortened. The child's foot is in danger of slipping right through and in the event of a fall he could be dragged. It is, of course, safer to punch extra holes in the leather, but as a temporary measure they can be shortened by unbuckling the leathers and making one turn around the top of the irons before buckling them up again.

The conformation of your prospective purchase is relatively unimportant if you do not intend to show the pony, except inasfar as it affects soundness. Temperament and manners are of the utmost importance in any child's first pony. Nevertheless, there is one aspect of conformation which should be considered. The pony should not be too broad in the back; a narrow pony is much more comfortable for a child to ride, and easier to sit on.

It is also an advantage if the pony has a 'good front', ie a sloping shoulder and well-developed withers, which enable the saddle to stay in the correct place. Ponies with short thick necks and no withers have nothing to prevent the saddle from sliding forward. Try to find a pony that is well balanced and doesn't carry its head too low. Children feel more secure if they can see something in front of them.

A child's first pony could make or mar his future interest in riding. It is important that the child should have every confidence in the animal and be encouraged to look after it himself. A super show pony is obviously very nice, but if the child is not allowed to look after it, he is not going to learn very much; and I wonder which child will be better equipped to cope with the inevitable disappointments and failures of a life with horses – the one who wins all the ribbons in the show ring, or the one who has to struggle hard to pick up a rosette in the potato race?

Children whose sole ambition it is to win rosettes in the show ring might like to read the following poem written by Will Ogilvie:

TO RIDERS OF THE SHOW RING

When the crowds are collected to cheer you
O'er the fences in front of the stand,
And when heaven itself would seem near you
And the ribbons are placed in your hand;
Your throne is not Caesar's or Nero's
The world is not all at your feet.
You're really no gallanter heroes
Than half of the others you've beat.

All the glory be pleased to remember
Was never intended to last
It will soon be no more than an ember
In the faded-out fires of the past.
There are lights that are brighter to borrow
There are flames that are finer to fan,
When you wake in the world of the morrow
And grow to be woman and man.

Be courtly to those you have beaten,
Be kindly to fellows who fall,
Disappointment's ill food to be eaten
Defeat can be bitter as gall.
Don't allow all those ribbons to spoil you
And behave as good breeding demands
And never let selfishness soil you
Or greed; they have dirt on their hands.

Be sportsmen and carry your honours
With pride, but with honesty too
And so be beloved by the donors
Who have handed their trophies to you.
Be kind to the rest you've outridden,
Be glad you've prevailed in the strife
And let jealousy die and be hidden
And you'll win the blue ribbons of Life!

13

Jumping

The ambition of most riders, especially children, is to learn to jump as soon as possible. The show jumping stars on the television make it look so simple that the fact that it has probably taken them years of dedicated hard work to reach that high standard is often overlooked.

From the safety point of view, however, you should not attempt to jump until you have attained a reasonable standard of riding ability. Accidents can happen merely because the rider's standard is not high enough to enable him to sit in the correct position over a fence, with the result that he either hangs on by the reins and jabs the horse in the mouth, or gets thrown out of the saddle. Before you jump, you should at least be able to ride reasonably well at all paces, have a firm seat independent of reins and stirrups, and be in complete control of your horse.

The jumping position

A horse that jumps without a rider is able to balance himself, but when the extra weight of a rider is placed on his back, his natural balance is upset and he finds it difficult to re-adjust, particularly if the rider is sitting in the wrong position. It is very important, therefore, that the rider interferes as little as possible with the movements of the horse, in particular with his head and neck, which he uses as a kind of balancing pole. By learning how to sit correctly over a fence, the rider is able to remain in balance and harmony with his horse throughout all phases of the jump – the approach, the take-off and the landing.

In order to appreciate fully the importance of the rider's position, it may be useful to study a horse jumping. Watch the horse as he canters into a fence, and you will see that immediately before leaving the ground he will lower his head and neck to

The correct jumping position

balance himself for the take-off. As he brings his hocks underneath him in order to thrust himself into the air, he raises his head, shortens his neck and lifts his forehand off the ground. In mid-air he stretches his head and neck forwards and down, tucks his front legs up and brings his hind legs up underneath him, like a plane gathering up its undercarriage. On coming to the ground he raises his head, again shortens his neck, and stretches his forelegs in front of him. Having studied each movement, you can now appreciate the value of placing yourself in the correct position, for both the horse's comfort and your own safety.

To get into the jumping position, incline your shoulders forward, bending from the hips with a straight but supple back and taking your weight on the knees and thighs, with the lower legs close to the horse's sides and the stirrup leathers hanging vertical. In order to maintain this position, you will find it necessary to shorten your stirrup leathers about two holes from the normal riding length.

Shorten the reins a little, and bend the arms slightly at the elbows so that a straight line is formed by the forearms, hands and reins to the horse's mouth. The contact with the mouth must be light and gentle, and as the horse stretches his head and neck your hands must follow the movement, allowing him the freedom to balance himself. It is important that this contact is maintained throughout; if you allow the reins to sag, not only

The result of standing in the stirrups and leaning too far forward

will you lose control of the horse, but it is one of the surest ways to induce a horse to refuse or run out (run past the fence instead of jumping it).

Avoid any tendency to stand up in the stirrups, as this will throw your weight forward, and in the event of a sudden refusal you will be catapulted over the horse's head.

Always remember to look up and ahead in the direction you wish to go. Looking down is a common fault amongst beginners, and has the effect of hunching the shoulders and pulling the seat forward out of the saddle. The closer your seat is to the saddle, the more control you will have over your horse.

Try to keep your whole body, including arms, shoulders and fingers, supple and flexible; any stiffness will be transferred through the reins to the horse's mouth, and will result in a dead feeling on the mouth instead of a soft give-and-take action.

Later on, when you become more experienced, you will find that you may be obliged to alter this basic position at times. For example, if you are riding a horse that is intent on refusing, you will have to bring your shoulders further back in order to make more use of your seat bones and legs to drive the horse forward on approaching the fence.

If you find it necessary to use your whip on a particularly sluggish horse in order to build up the necessary impulsion, the reins must be taken in one hand and the position of the whip hand changed, so that the thumb is pointing downwards to enable you to obtain a firmer grip. The whip should not be used to punish, but as a reminder to 'wake up and pay attention'. Use it decisively just behind your leg, not on the horse's shoulder where it may cause him to swerve away from it and run out. It should not be used during the last three strides of the approach to the fence unless the rider is very experienced, as the balance of both horse and rider will be upset.

I have recently noticed several show jumpers, particularly children, holding their whips 'upside down', that is, with the whole length of the whip pointing upwards across the front of the rider's body. From a safety point of view this could be disastrous, as it is not only distracting for the horse, but the rider is in danger of having the whip poked in his eye.

In more advanced jumping, the expert can shorten or lengthen his horse's stride during the approach so that the horse will take off at a point chosen by the rider. Here again the use of the seat bones is most important, and the 'jumping position' is actually taken up only as the horse leaves the ground.

To avoid confusion, however, the beginner will find it easier to stay in the jumping position throughout all phases of the jump. For this reason, it is essential that the horse that is chosen for the first lessons is an experienced jumper who will jump willingly and freely, and will not be likely either to refuse or get excited, so that the rider is able to concentrate entirely on his own position.

The neck strap

A useful item which can be of assistance to the novice rider is a neck strap, which is placed around the horse's neck and can be held if the rider feels unsafe. A stirrup leather or the neck strap of a martingale will serve the purpose very well. Care must be taken, however, to ensure that the rider does not come to rely on it for support, but uses it only in the initial lessons to help him keep his weight forward as the horse takes off in front of a fence.

An important point to remember is that the neck strap can only be held with one hand, as the other hand will be holding

the reins; the rein hand, of course, must be held in front of the
other one, allowing it full freedom to slide forward as the horse
stretches his neck. On no account should the reins and neck
strap be held in the same hand or in both hands, as this would
prevent the reins from following the movement of the horse's
head.

If a neck strap is not available, holding a lock of the horse's
mane serves the same purpose. Again, the hand holding the
reins must be in front of the one holding the mane.

Preparing for your first jump

An effective way of preparing yourself for jumping is to get
your horse to trot over some poles laid on the ground. Some of
the better-equipped riding schools have specially designed poles
called *cavalletti* which are about 10ft (3m) long and are attached
to cross-pieces at each end. These poles can be adjusted to three
different heights – 10in (25cm), 15in (38cm) or 19in (48cm) –
merely by rolling them over. They are placed at varying distances
apart, depending on the size of the horse and the pace at which
it is moving. For instance, when placed at their lowest height
and about 4–5ft (1.2–1.5m) apart, they are correctly spaced for
a horse to trot over them. It is important that you do not increase
the height for the trot, as the horse will not be able to negotiate
them correctly. You must have a horse that is experienced in
cavalletti work, and you will find that he will trot over the
poles in long rhythmic strides, giving you an opportunity to
practise your jumping position as you ride over them.

If *cavalletti* are not available, ordinary thick poles such as
jumping poles will be perfectly adequate; to prevent them from
rolling about, nail a piece of board to each end. In order to
increase the height you can lay the ends on bricks, which can
be added to as required.

As soon as you are able to sit correctly at the trot, increase
the height to 15in (38cm) and spread the poles so that they are
18–20ft (5.5–6m) apart, which is the correct distance for
cantering. At this spacing the horse will take one canter stride

between each pole, and the effect will be similar to a series of tiny jumps.

When you feel really secure and confident, raise the *cavalletti* or poles to their maximum height of 19in (48cm) and decrease the spacing between them to 9–10ft (2.7–3m). At this distance the horse will be obliged to 'bounce' over them, ie he will have to jump each one without taking a canter stride in between.

All this practice over poles will give you some idea of what a real jump feels like – in fact you will scarcely know the difference.

The early jumps

You are now ready to start jumping small fences, which you can build yourself. Materials such as oil drums, old tyres, gorse, coloured poles, sand bags etc can all be used to produce a variety of jumps. Try to make the fences as solid as possible; if they are too flimsy the horse will soon lose respect for them, and may start brushing through them.

Place your fences where the ground is neither too stony, too hard nor too boggy. A lot of leg trouble in horses is caused by jumping them on hard ground, where the front legs are jarred on landing. If the ground is too soft, on the other hand, the horse's hocks are liable to be strained as he takes off.

To prevent the horse from getting too close to the fence and having to make an awkward jump (cat-jump), place a pole, some gorse or branches or anything similar in front of the jump, about the same distance away from it as the height of the fence, or a little further in the case of a low one. This will encourage the horse to stand back and jump in the correct manner, forming an arc, or 'parabola', as the show jumpers call it.

Always ensure that every fence is perfectly safe for the horse to jump. A carelessly built one may contain all kinds of hazards. There is no guarantee that your horse will clear it every time, so make sure that there is nothing on which he could injure himself – rusty nails or sharp projections – or anything in which he could get a foot trapped. If you are using standard show jumps, remember to remove any spare 'cups' (the metal holders placed on the wings to support the poles) if they are not being used to hold a pole. These often have sharp edges, and both you and your horse risk a nasty gash if you jump too close to a wing.

Do not get too ambitious and build your fences too high at first. It is better, both for your horse and yourself, to use your imagination in building a variety of jumps than to make them too high and risk encouraging the horse to refuse. If you want to make them more difficult, increase the spread but not the height.

Never jump anything – a gate, for example – that is leaning towards you. If the horse hits it, he will force it higher before it can fall.

If you are enjoying yourself, it is a great temptation to go on and on jumping. Resist it! Endless repetition will sour your horse and eventually make him reluctant to jump.

Until you gain more experience, never ride too fast at your fences. Give the horse plenty of time to balance himself, and yourself time to concentrate on your position. Practise jumping some of them from a trot.

If the horse runs out, turn him round in the opposite direction – ie, if he goes to the left, turn him back towards the right – and when you try the fence again, ride him at a slight angle from the left to the righthand side of the fence.

Make jumping a pleasure for the horse

It is obvious that you must not jump your horse unless he is absolutely sound. If, for example, there is even slight heat or swelling in any leg, although he may not actually be lame, it is safer not to jump him, as you will only aggravate the trouble.

The same, of course, applies to the horse that needs shoeing. A lot of damage can be done to the foot if, for instance, the horse is jumped when it is too long, or when the hoof is growing over the edges of the shoe, causing the shoe to press into the heel.

If your horse is going to enjoy his jumping – and he will soon let you know if he doesn't, by refusing – he must be comfortable.

Always check your tack and make sure that it fits before you begin. A saddle with the pommel pressing on the withers, or a bit banging against the horse's teeth, can be very painful (see pp. 23–30).

The novice should never use any type of severe bit, for example a curb, which has a chain fitted around the horse's chin groove to enable the bit to act as a lever (see the diagram on p. 105). There are of course a great many different types of bit, too numerous to mention here, but as a general rule the beginner should use one of the less severe types such as the plain snaffle. It must be borne in mind, however, that even the snaffle can be extremely painful to the horse if handled roughly. You may say, 'That's all very well, but I can't hold my horse in a snaffle.' In that case, the horse is not a suitable one on which to learn, and should be handed over to an experienced rider.

As I have tried to stress in the chapter on handling young horses, if the rider has 'good hands' (sensitive and sympathetic), his horse will come to no harm in the most severe of bits, but if the opposite applies, the horse's mouth can be damaged even in a mild bit. Good hands, of course, depend on a firm and balanced seat, and as this takes time to acquire, the novice rider could not be expected to handle anything but the simplest of bits. In fact, he should never attempt to use any complicated piece of tack that he does not understand or is not fully capable of handling.

Both horses and ponies must be amazingly long-suffering: the way some of them are thoughtlessly over-jumped, over-ridden, and generally hauled around at shows and gymkhanas, it is remarkable that they ever jump at all. Jumping should be made a pleasure for them, and at the end of a good round they deserve a few generous pats and kind words. Like dogs, they are quick to recognise the difference between approval and anger in your voice.

14

Safety in the Hunting Field

Whether you agree with hunting or are bitterly against it, there is no doubt that it often reveals the characters of those who take part in it. It is a testing ground, not only of physical courage and riding ability, but of other qualities such as self-control, good manners, unselfishness, good humour and, above all, consideration for your horse's needs before your own.

In the excitement of a fast run across country and the desire to be up with hounds, which of us has never been tempted to take a short cut across forbidden territory; to pretend not to see a loose horse; to push in front of someone at a fence; to ignore a fallen rider; or to ride a horse beyond his limit when we know he has had enough? Each rider's behaviour can affect not only his own safety, but that of everyone else, so it is the responsibility of everyone concerned to ride with care and thought for others.

Many hunting accidents could be avoided with a little more consideration and common sense. For example, some people who get kicked have only themselves to blame, because they allow their horses to get too close to others. One often sees a rider slopping along on a loose rein with his horse stepping on the heels of the one in front who, quite naturally, shows his resentment by lashing out. Of course, there are situations where it is impossible not to crowd together, as in a narrow lane or when going through a gateway, but by keeping alert, and watching other horses for signs of bad temper – laying back the ears, for example – many accidents can be avoided.

It must be remembered that hunting often has a stimulating effect on horses. Even the old stagers may get excited at the start of the day, and behave in a manner that would be quite foreign to them away from the hunting field.

Preparing for your first meet

Before you go hunting, it is important that you have enough confidence in your ability to control your horse in these exciting circumstances. The standard of riding required is a little higher than that needed for merely hacking around the roads.

A rider who loses control of his horse out hunting is a danger, not only to himself and the rest of the 'field' (other riders), but also to the hounds. One of the worst crimes you can commit is to kick or over-ride hounds. It is, of course, difficult to assess beforehand how your horse will behave, but he will soon give you an indication once you start hunting, and if you realise that he is going to be too much of a handful, take him home; you can always try again when you have gained more riding experience.

Read as much as you can about hunting before you go out. It would be ideal if you could find a knowledgeable person who would be willing to help you, and guide you through your first day with hounds. There is so much to learn about correct behaviour, hunting terms, the Master, the Hunt Staff, the hounds, the crops and the countryside that an experienced mentor would be a great asset.

From the safety point of view, it would be sensible to choose carefully the venue of your first meet. For instance, choose a place where there is likely to be a minimum of followers. Any member of the hunt will be able to tell you which meet would be

Riding too close to the horse in front

most suitable. The Opening Meet (first meet of the foxhunting season held at the beginning of November) usually attracts a large crowd, not only of riders, but of foot and car followers and also casual sightseers. Any difficulties the beginner might have will be increased by the presence of a lot of horses, and the exciting atmosphere.

It would probably be better, at first, for the novice to attend some of the 'cubbing' meets, which take place during September and October when the number of followers will be less, and the pace slower. This is the period when the huntsman trains the young hounds.

Study the type of country and the fences that you may be required to jump. It is not obligatory to jump, of course, but you will soon lose the hounds if you are unable to do so. Hunting country varies considerably from one area to another; try to choose somewhere that has the type of fences with which you are familiar.

Getting the horse fit

If you intend to hunt regularly, and expect your horse to stay out all day, it is most important that he is carefully prepared and conditioned beforehand. Irreparable damage can be done to his wind and legs if he is hunted when not fully fit. Horses that have been turned out to grass for the summer months are often too fat, and need at least six weeks to get them into hunting condition. The process must obviously be a gradual one. A sudden change of diet and a lot of fast exercise could result in colic, indigestion, filled legs and damaged lungs.

When the horse is first brought into the stable, he must have plenty of fresh air – leave the top half of the door open. Coughs often start, when horses are brought up from grass, as a result of a stuffy stable and too much dry food. At first his diet should consist mainly of hay and damp bran, with a few oats or horse cubes (see chapter 6). During the first fortnight he will not need more than about 4lb (1.8kg) of oats or cubes and about 8lb (3.6kg) of bran per day. This should be divided into three or preferably four feeds. The addition of something succulent such as carrots, apples, mangolds, turnips etc will give variety and do him good. Unless he is the sort of horse who gets over-fat, he can be given as much hay as he will eat, but give the bulk of it after exercise rather than before.

He will need walking exercise only for the first few days; in fact some people will not allow their horses to go out of a walk for at least two weeks. The longer that slow work is continued the better, of course, but a few short periods of trotting will not harm him, as long as he is not blowing or sweating. Make sure that he is absolutely dry and cool when he is brought back to the stable. At this stage he will sweat very quickly and will be liable to catch a chill if left in the stable in a lather of sweat. An hour's exercise is sufficient at first, but as the horse becomes fitter he can be kept out for longer periods.

Gradually reduce his bran ration and increase the oats or cubes until, by the time he is ready to hunt, he is receiving about 8–10lb (3.6–4.5kg) of oats and 4lb (1.8kg) of bran per day. These amounts are only a very rough guide; exact quantities, as usual, will depend entirely on the type of horse, his size, temperament and appetite, and your own ability to control him. If you find that he is getting too fresh, then the amount of oats will have to be reduced and his bran ration increased accordingly. Certain horses tend to get fat easily, and consequently must have less hay, while others never seem to put on weight, and should have all the hay they can eat.

Some safety rules

The majority of 'dos' and 'don'ts' which apply in the hunting field really depend on good manners and consideration for others. For example, never barge into other riders in order to get through a gateway first, or gallop wildly past someone who is obviously riding a young or excitable horse. The latter point should be noted particularly by children, who are often thoughtless in this respect. Young horses who are not used to ponies can become really upset, and may endanger their riders by bucking

A pony startling a young horse by rushing thoughtlessly past

or rearing, if small ponies suddenly hurtle past them. Quite often the young riders of the ponies are completely oblivious of the havoc they are causing.

Keep alert, and avoid getting into situations that could be dangerous. For example, learn to recognise individual horses so that you can keep out of the way of those that are likely to kick, those that the rider has difficulty in holding, and young horses that may be unpredictable. If a rider knows that his horse is prone to kicking, he should tie a red ribbon on his tail as a warning to others; but this will not excuse him if he allows his horse to kick someone.

Get your horse used to the sound of a hunting crop (whip) being cracked before you take him hunting. Someone may suddenly crack his whip nearby, and if your horse is not accustomed to it he may be upset. He must also get used to the thong being dangled around his hind legs, as this is sometimes necessary to keep hounds away from the horse's heels. If he is nervous, take your whip with you while exercising and practise cracking it, very gently at first, until he takes no notice of it.

Be careful, when you take your sandwiches out to eat them, that the rustle of the paper does not startle your horse. It is surprising how often little details like this are overlooked.

Never jump too close to the horse in front of you; if he falls, or the rider comes off, your horse may trample on them. Also make sure that you do not cut in front of a rider who is approaching a fence : he may not be able to avoid cannoning into you, and his horse could be turned against jumping for a long time.

Accidents sometimes occur because a rider allows a gate to swing back into the face of the horse that is following him. Be very careful to look behind and hold a swinging gate until the next rider is able to catch it and prevent it from trapping his horse against the gatepost. If someone dismounts to open a gate, wait until he is safely mounted again before you move off. If hounds are running and everyone is galloping through the gateway, it is not only courteous, but the duty, of the last person through to wait behind and help the person who has opened the gate – his horse may be excited and difficult to mount when he sees his companions galloping away from him. It is important, of course, that all gates are securely latched.

Keep an eye on the hounds whenever possible. Never ride too close to them, either while they are hunting or when you are hacking along the road behind them. If you meet the pack in a narrow lane, turn your horse's head towards them and push his hindquarters close to the hedge so that he cannot kick. Do not allow him to lower his head to sniff at the hounds as they pass – he may try to bite, or strike them with a front foot.

Courtesy

The importance of good manners when out hunting cannot be overstressed. It takes only one rude, arrogant rider to ruin the good name of the whole hunt. It must never be forgotten that we ride across the farmer's land by his courtesy alone; it is a privilege, and not a right. The landowner who objects to the hunt coming on to his land must be treated with the utmost respect; he probably has many reasons for his objection. A swift apology and a smile, if you inadvertently trespass, will do much more to restore goodwill than an argument.

Never ride across any field that has been sown with a crop, nor any that has been cultivated and rolled but in which the crop has not yet begun to grow. The pits that are made by horse's hoofs, especially on a wet day, can do a lot of damage. You can, of course, easily distinguish such crops as potatoes, kale, cauliflower and turnips, but you may need to learn to recognise young wheat, winter oats, barley or recently sown grass. The young grass and clover which grow up between the stubble left behind from the cereal crop are known as 'seeds', and these too must be avoided.

Be courteous, too, to anyone using a public highway, whether drivers or pedestrians. A group of riders chatting together in the middle of a road, heedless of cars waiting to pass, can be very annoying to someone who is in a hurry. An incident which happened recently illustrates this point very clearly. I was riding a young horse along the road when a baker's van came tearing up behind me. I signalled to him to slow down, whereupon he skidded to a halt in front of me, jumped out of his van and shouted angrily, saying that I had no right to ask him to slow down on a public highway. After a rather heated exchange, in which I tried to explain the danger of frightening a young horse, it transpired that he had just been held up on the road by 'a lot of rude, arrogant people on horses, with dogs running all over the place', who simply ignored his plea to give him room to pass. Apparently he had had the misfortune to run into the local hunt, whose manners, it seems, on that occasion had left a lot to be desired. Having heard the reason for his behaviour, I saw the incident from his point of view and could sympathise with his attitude. Nevertheless, in his justifiable anger and frustration he could have injured both my horse and me.

Good manners are the result of kind hearts. If you see someone in trouble out hunting, go and help him. Try to catch a loose horse if a rider falls off, or hold a fidgety one if someone is having difficulty in mounting. Go out of your way to be friendly, particularly to anyone whom you know to be a stranger to the hunt and is not familiar with the country.

It is important also to be courteous to the Master and Hunt Staff. Make a point of saying 'good morning' when you arrive at the meet, and remember to thank them at the end of the day.

Never get into the habit of criticising the Master, the Huntsman or the hounds, or generally running down your hunt. Hunting a pack of hounds is an extremely difficult and exacting job, and you do not always know all the circumstances. The Master and Hunt Staff need all the support and co-operation that they can get if they are to be a success. By continually criticising, you do the hunt a disservice.

It may seem that I have harped on the subject of good manners, but without them hunting would soon become a rabble, and many young riders would be discouraged.

Jumping fences

A great deal of the fun of hunting comes from jumping fences. It is often difficult to resist the temptation to jump unnecessarily, but if hounds are not running, avoid it where possible and go through the gate. Your horse may not do any damage to the fence, but others are bound to follow you, and after a dozen or more horses have jumped, the damage could be considerable.

When hounds are running, you have a legitimate excuse to jump, in order to stay with them. No one, of course, can avoid the occasional fall, but generally speaking your safety will depend a great deal on the way you ride. Each fence has to be ridden differently according to its height and breadth, the state of the take-off and landing, and so on. For example, if you were jumping a fence with a wide ditch on the landing side you would have to ride your horse faster, in order to gain the necessary momentum to clear it, than if you were perhaps jumping an upright fence or one with a big drop on the landing side, where greater precision is required.

Horses become accustomed to the fences in their own particular country, and it is always safer to ride a horse who knows how to negotiate them. In West Cornwall, for instance, the horses have to learn how to jump on and off a narrow bank. These must be approached slowly, usually from a trot, so that the horse has time to balance himself and place all four feet on the top of the bank. Gates, stone walls, post-and-rail fences and any fence into water must also be approached fairly slowly

– at the canter rather than the gallop – in order to achieve more accuracy.

If you need to check your horse, do not do so within the last few yards of the approach to the fence, but well before – at least twenty yards – so that the horse is free to lower his head and balance himself at the point of take-off.

When jumping into a slippery road, jump at an angle in the direction you wish to go. For instance, if you want to turn to the left on landing, then jump towards the left as you take off so that you will not be obliged to turn sharply and run the risk of your horse slipping up.

A final word concerning jumping. When the day's hunting is over, do not be tempted to jump fences on the way home. Accidents are more likely to happen then than at any other time. Your horse is tired, and beginning to lose concentration; his lack of interest will encourage him to refuse, or he may hit the fence through sheer fatigue.

Put your horse first

If you value your horse, do not hunt him while he is too young. A great deal of damage can be inflicted on a young horse's legs by hard riding before the bones and muscles have had time to mature. Horses ought not to be hunted until they are four years old, and even then should not stay out all day. A horse is not 'grown up' until he is five or six years old, and cannot be expected to stand up to the many stresses and strains of a long day's hunting until he reaches the age of maturity. Many accidents with young horses are caused by over-tiredness. They are not fully fit, and consequently start dragging their legs over the fences, with the obvious results.

I wonder sometimes just how many horses stand dejectedly in their boxes on the day after hunting with scarred, swollen legs, perhaps taking weeks to recover, when with a little unselfishness and care on the part of the rider they could have been taken home much earlier in the day and saved the extra strain and risk that a long day imposes. Remember that all the mental excitement of hunting can cause just as much strain and fatigue to a young horse as the physical part of it.

You can do a lot to ensure your own safety by looking after your horse. As I have said, quite a number of accidents happen because the horse is tired and not physically capable of jumping big fences in that condition. To expect a horse to hunt all day if he is not a hundred per cent fit is asking for trouble. Do remember that horses are not machines. You can fill a car with petrol and expect it to run until the tank is empty, but don't expect the same principle to work with a horse just because you fill him with oats!

There are many ways in which you can assist your horse to conserve his energy during a day's hunting.

1 Do not gallop flat out on soft going such as ploughland or boggy places, but keep the horse well in hand and slow up. Where possible, ride round the edge of a ploughed field instead of across it.

2 Watch carefully for pits and rough patches of ground.

3 Never gallop on public roads. Not only will it jar your horse's legs, but it is dangerous for other road users.

4 If you feel that your horse is tiring, use your discretion, and don't ask him to jump the highest part of the fence.

5 Keep an eye on the leading hounds – you may see that they are swinging left or right, and in some cases it might be possible to take a short cut, though you must make sure that you do not get in front of them or in any way impede their progress.

6 Get to know the country. You can save your horse a lot of galloping by knowing exactly where the fences are safe to jump, or perhaps where certain crossing places are, or the land over which you are not allowed to ride.

If you are unfortunate enough to have a fall, check your horse carefully before mounting again to make sure that he has not suffered any injury.

After a run, dismount and loosen the girth; shift the saddle around on the horse's back to allow the air to get underneath, and check that no thorns have worked their way underneath the saddle.

If the horse loses a shoe, it is sensible to take him home before he damages his foot. The hoof will be liable to crack, and will wear away very quickly, particularly on stony ground.

Going home

If your horse has had a hard day, give him a chance to unwind on the way home. Let him walk on a long rein so that he can stretch his neck and ease aching muscles. This does not imply that you should ride with loose, drooping reins; you must still be in complete control by keeping light contact with the horse's mouth.

Let him have a drink if you can find some clean water on the way. A study of veterinary books reveals that the feeling of fatigue in a horse is due to the formation of certain poisons, and it is essential for a tired horse to drink in order to get rid of these waste products.

If you get off and walk the last mile, loosening the girth and shifting the saddle, the horse's back should be dry by the time he gets back to the stable.

Although taking the horse home in a horse box or trailer has obvious advantages, it also poses certain problems. One of these is the question of how many rugs to put on. The greatest danger, after a horse has been sweating a lot, is that of catching a chill. He must not be allowed to get cold; but on the other hand, if you rug him up too much in the box he will arrive home in a lather of sweat. The final answer will depend, of course, on the weather, the draughtiness of the box and whether the horse gets cold easily or sweats easily. You can only decide by trial and error, and by getting to know your own particular horse. The use of an anti-sweat rug, either by itself or underneath another rug, may solve the problem (see p. 81).

Some people like to leave the saddle on until the horse gets home, but there is always the risk that the horse may rub against the side of the box and damage the saddle. I find that if you remove the saddle, and give the back a brisk rub with the hands to restore the circulation, it will be quite dry by the time you get home. Always remove the bridle and put on a headcollar. If the horse has some hay in a net to munch at, he will be more relaxed on the journey.

I do not believe in bandaging the legs at this stage, for two reasons. Firstly, you may well bandage over a thorn and force it further into the leg, and secondly, while you are fussing around with bandages the horse will have to stand still, quite often in a cold wind, and could easily catch a chill.

Care of horse after hunting

On returning to the stable, the horse should be made comfortable as quickly and with as little fuss as possible, so that he can relax and rest. Make sure that his bedding is down so that he will be encouraged to stale; some horses object to doing it in a horse box.

There has always been a certain amount of controversy as to the correct treatment of a horse after hunting, and even those with a lifetime's experience will disagree amongst themselves. It is all very confusing to the novice, but I think the true answer lies in studying each individual horse and his particular needs.

Water
Some people maintain that the water given to a horse after hunting should have the chill taken off to prevent colic. Others, including some vets, say that this is neither necessary nor desirable. Personally, I have never known a horse to have colic as a result of drinking cold water.

It may be of interest here to quote from the book *Stable Management and Exercise* by Captain M. H. Hayes, FRCVS, who spent two winters in Northern Russia. He says:

In that country, during winter, all the common horses, such as cab and cart animals, are habitually given icy cold water, and no attempt is ever made to warm it for them . . . Throughout my long life, which has been spent among horses in all kinds of climates, and in many different parts of the world, I have never known, heard, or read of a case of injury to a horse, caused by the fact of the water he drank being cold.

However, as I have tried to stress, horses are individuals, and something that affects one may not affect another. I know of one particular mare who, if she is given a lot of cold water after a hard day's hunting, will immediately start shivering; if the chill is taken off, this does not happen. This case, though, seems to be the exception, and provided the horse is kept warm afterwards, cold water will do no harm.

Horses should never be deprived of water for long periods, and a few mouthfuls snatched from a river or any clean source while hunting would help to prevent them from drinking too much on arrival home. A few mouthfuls would not be enough to harm the horse, even if he was required to do fast work immediately afterwards.

Grooming

If the horse's legs and abdomen are still wet and muddy, rub the worst of it off with a handful of straw, being very careful to inspect the legs for any thorns, cuts or scratches which, of course, must be attended to immediately (see chapter 9). Then allow the legs to dry. Some people hasten the drying process by putting on old flannel bandages over a layer of straw. This is not a good idea if there are any cuts, as the straw will not only hurt, but will be full of germs. Hosing the legs is not recommended, as it may give rise to cracked heels and mud fever (inflammation of the skin covering legs and heels), particularly if they are not meticulously dried afterwards.

Ensure that the saddle mark (hair left unclipped underneath the saddle) is thoroughly dried.

Pick out the feet, and see that there are no stones or gravel embedded in the soles.

If the horse is inclined to break out (see p. 81), either put an anti-sweat rug underneath the night rug, or put a layer of straw on the back, with the night rug on top. Both have the effect of trapping warm air, which allows the horse to cool down slowly, without catching a chill.

Feeding
When a horse is tired, his powers of digestion are impaired and he is unable to digest hard, dry food such as oats. After hunting he should be given a bran and linseed mash (see p. 75), which is warming, very easy to digest, and is relished by most horses. After feeding him, hang up his haynet and leave him in peace while you clean off your tack and have your own meal.

Final visit to the stable
It is most important that you return later to make sure he has eaten his feed, to brush off the remaining dry mud, and to see that he is dry and warm. If he has broken out, he must be thoroughly dried with a wisp or piece of towelling, particularly round the loin area, where he is liable to get a chill in the kidneys. His ears will probably be cold and wet, and these can be dried quite quickly by gently pulling them through the fingers.

Finally, put on stable bandages to keep his legs warm. This will help the circulation and prevent them from swelling.

Check his water bucket and haynet; make sure both are full. Now that he has had time to recover, he can be given a last small feed of oats (2–3lb, or 0.9–1.4kg), and then you have finished for the night.

15

Safety in Handling
Young Horses

A young horse is rather like an unexploded bomb – handle him carefully and you will be reasonably safe, but make one sudden or unexpected move and he may blow up in your face!

There seems to be an increasing trend these days for people with little or no experience of horses to buy young ones and attempt to break them in. Many accidents occur because people simply do not realise what can happen if they do the wrong thing. As I have tried to stress throughout the book, safety lies in knowledge and understanding of the horse's mentality. Young horses panic very quickly, and when fear is uppermost all else is forgotten. For example, someone who has never broken in a horse before may put the saddle on in the normal way and buckle up the girth, expecting the horse to stand still as he would if he had been ridden for some time. Instead, that person may be surprised to see the hitherto docile animal erupt into an equine volcano!

It should be remembered that, in the days of our ancestors, the wild horse was often attacked by wolves, lions and other predators which would leap on to his back and cling there until they could sink their teeth into his neck for the kill. It is quite understandable, therefore, that the instinct of self-preservation is still there and that the young horse will buck, rear or kick to dislodge any strange object that he feels on his back. In much the same way, he will feel trapped if he is suddenly tied so that he cannot get away, and will exhibit the same tactics of self-preservation.

These are only two of the dangers that a novice might encounter if he had insufficient knowledge to avoid them; there are many, many more. It is reasonable, then, to assert that a young horse or pony should only be handled by an experienced person.

Training young horses successfully is something that cannot be accomplished by merely reading books on the subject; it should only be attempted after some years of practical experience. Inevitably, though, there will be some who will not be deterred, and will still wish to train a horse of their own. I hope, then, that this chapter may be of some help to those whose knowledge of young horses is limited and who have no one to whom they can turn for help, particularly to those who have perhaps bought or bred a foal and would like to rear and eventually break it in themselves.

Handling foals

A horse's whole future depends on the way in which he is handled in early life. His attitude to mankind and his behaviour throughout his formative years will be affected by the type of person responsible for his upbringing. Like that of a child, the character of a horse is formed in early youth, and once spoiled he will be very difficult to retrain.

A foal's training should really begin on the day he is born. The most important lesson that you can teach him – and one, incidentally, that will help to ensure your future safety – is that he has nothing to fear. As I have said, a frightened horse is a potentially dangerous one.

Always approach him slowly and deliberately. When reaching out to stroke him, do so very quietly, with no sudden movements of the arm. (Never pat a foal – the jerky action will startle him.) Do not forget that he has just entered a strange and bewildering world, and that it will take time for him to gain trust and confidence in human beings. Gradually get him accustomed to being handled all over his body, including his legs.

A few days after the birth, put on a foal slip. This is a small halter made especially for foals, and it is important that it is kept soft and pliable so that it does not rub the foal's head. Make sure it fits snugly but not too tightly : if it is too small it will

The foal slip

prevent him from using his jaws properly, and if too big, the foal is liable to put a foot through it while scratching his ears with a hind foot. He could also get it hooked on some projection. It is safer to remove it if the foal is not under supervision.

A word of warning here! A foal's head grows quite quickly, and the halter must be adjusted accordingly. A dead foal was once found on Dartmoor with the halter embedded in its swollen head. Unable to move its jaws, it had died of starvation, simply because someone had forgotten to adjust the size of its halter.

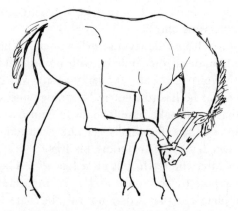

A foal with his hind leg caught in a slip which is too large for him

Teaching the foal to lead

The foal should be taught to lead within a few days of birth. Attach a lead rope to the slip, and let him walk close to his mother at first. It helps if you can get someone else to lead the mare and allow the foal to follow. If he resists the lead rope, place your arm around his buttocks and partly push him forward. It is important that you do not put too much strain on his young neck at this stage. Gradually increase the distance from the mare until eventually you are able to lead the foal away from her, in the opposite direction. Be firm, but never punish or shout at him; after all, he is only doing what nature intended him to do – that is, to escape from captivity.

Foals handled quietly and taught to lead in this gradual way will be far less frightened than those who are not taught to lead until they are weaned, by which time they have become too strong for one person to handle. It is a grim sight to see two or three men dragging a half-demented yearling round and round a field while the poor thing rears and struggles at the end of a rope. Not only is the animal likely to get injured in the process, but it is an unnerving experience that no youngster should be forced to endure. Unfortunately, it happens much too often, and there have been several cases where the colt has fallen over backwards and broken its neck.

There is no need for a horse to be frightened at any stage of his training; if he is, there is something wrong with the system. You may say that you haven't the time to spend with a foal in the way that I have described : in that case, think very hard before either buying or breeding one.

Catching the foal

If the mare is easy to catch, the foal, as he grows older and begins to trust you, will be the same. When he begins to nibble at his dam's oats, feed him some from your hand each time he comes to you in the field, and you will soon have no trouble catching him.

I am always a little suspicious of people who complain that their horses are difficult to catch : either the horse associates being caught with something unpleasant, or for some reason he does not trust his owner.

Weaning

When a foal is taken away from his mother at the age of about six months, he is liable to be extremely frightened, and unless you are very careful he will injure himself trying to get back to her. If at all possible, it is a good idea to find a companion for him, such as an old pony, another foal that is ready to be weaned, or even a goat. If this is impractical, make sure the field where he is to be turned out is absolutely stock-proof, and that there is nothing on which the foal could hurt himself. The mare must be taken out of earshot, otherwise both will go frantic neighing at each other. It is probably wiser to keep the foal in for a day or two until he settles down, but don't shut him away in some dark shed – let him see what is going on. A grid in place of the top half of the stable door will prevent him from jumping out, but at the same time let the light in and allow the foal to view his surroundings.

The yearling

By this time your youngster should be quiet to handle, easy to lead, and used to having his feet picked up. He should also have had his feet kept in good shape by the blacksmith. Tying up should present no problem, but always be prepared in case he pulls back, and be ready to release him before he injures himself. Never leave a young horse tied up on his own; if he panicked he could break his neck.

Now is the time to lay the foundation of good manners that will help to ensure your future safety. Teach him to stand still when asked. This is an important lesson, and if learned thoroughly will be a great asset to you in his future training. Always use the same word, 'stand' or 'whoa' or whatever you prefer, so that he begins to recognise the sound. Only by constant repetition and reward for obedience will you obtain results. A pat and a few soft words, *immediately* he does what you ask, will be reward enough. Don't make a habit of giving titbits, as he will start nibbling at you and will not concentrate on the lesson. An occasional carrot at the end of the session will do no harm.

Never shout or lose your temper if he fails to understand. Training any animal takes endless patience, and if you have not got it in abundance, you will never be able to teach even the most simple lesson. Do not expect too much – some horses are very much slower to learn than others. As Jorrocks tells us, 'The less a man knows about an 'oss, the more he expects.'

First encounters with traffic
At this stage it is an excellent idea to accustom the young horse to traffic, farm tractors, pigs, cattle, sheep and so on. Lead him around quiet country lanes and through farmyards (with the permission of the farmer). Take him to the intersection of a main road where there is plenty of room – a grass verge, for example, where he can stand in safety and watch cars and lorries pass without being frightened. All this will pay dividends later on when you start to ride him on the roads. Many accidents would be avoided if horses were given more time to become familiar with all these strange sights and sounds before being ridden.

Manners in the stable
Stable manners are very important, and a vital part of a horse's training. He should learn to move over on command and to stand still when you ask. Never allow him to barge through the stable door as soon as it is opened; teach him to stand there with the door open until you allow him to move. All this training instils discipline and the habit of obedience. You will find that when the time comes to ride him, your horse will be quiet, confident, obedient, and much safer to ride than one who has had no preliminary training.

Lungeing

When your horse is three years old it is time to begin his serious

The position in which the trainer should stand when lungeing

schooling. Some people like to start earlier, but a younger horse is very immature; his joints and tendons are easily strained, he tires quickly, and, like a young child, he will not concentrate for any length of time. Even at three years old he is still a baby, and nothing very strenuous should be asked of him. A horse or pony is not fully mature until he is five years old.

One of the first lessons he will have to learn is how to be lunged. To put it simply, this means asking the horse to circle round you while you stand in the middle holding him on the end of a rope or lunge rein. In this way you can teach him to obey commands to walk, trot, halt etc; get him supple by asking him to circle left and right; help him to develop physically by giving him exercise without requiring him to carry a weight on his back; and teach him to go forward with long, even strides.

If you have had no previous experience of lungeing a horse, it is essential that you find someone to demonstrate correctly. You can do a lot of harm to a young horse, both mentally and physically, if you are unsure of yourself, and a serious accident could occur if he became entangled in the lunge rein.

Equipment
You will need a lungeing cavesson, which is a type of headcollar with a heavy, padded metal noseband. It has three rings, one on each side, and one in the front of the noseband for the attachment of the lunge rein. This rigid noseband gives much more control than an ordinary headcollar.

The lunge rein, about 25ft (7.5m) long, is made of soft hemp or nylon and has a snap hook or buckle mounted on a swivel to prevent the rein from twisting. If you do not want to go to the expense of buying a rein, a piece of lightweight rope such as a plough line will be perfectly adequate.

You will also need a lungeing whip, which is a long lightweight whip used to prevent the horse from coming into the centre of the circle, and to drive him gently forward if need be. Again, these whips are expensive, and a long piece of bamboo makes a very good substitute.

For extra protection, it is wise to put bandages or boots on the horse's legs to prevent injury. A young horse is inclined to knock himself until he learns to handle his legs properly. For your own protection, always wear gloves. If the horse tries to pull away from you, they will protect your hands from rope burns, which can be very painful. Never twist the rein or rope around your hand; if the horse bolted, you could be dragged.

Preparing to lunge
First of all, ensure that the cavesson fits correctly. The noseband should not be too low, where it will cause the horse pain and irritation. It should lie about three fingers' width below the cheekbone, and be tight enough to prevent it from twisting on the horse's head. The jowl straps (side straps) should also be fastened fairly tightly, so that the cheekpieces do not get into the horse's eyes.

Some horses with sensitive noses object to having the lunge rein on the front of the noseband, and will shake their heads and refuse to go forward quietly. If this happens, attach the rein to the back of the noseband. You will not have the same measure of control, but the horse will go forward more freely.

You will soon learn how strong your horse is and whether you can control him without any trouble.

If you are lucky enough to have the use of an indoor school, that would be an ideal place to give the first few lessons. Most of us, however, have to be content with a small paddock or corner of a field. If using a field, choose a quiet corner where you can utilise the two hedges to form part of the rough boundary of your circle. Always remember to close the gate; if the horse does succeed in getting away from you, at least he will be confined to the field.

Circling

To start the horse moving on the lunge, lead him round in small circles to the left or right – you will probably find the left more convenient to start with, as your whip will be in the right hand – and then gradually pay out more and more lunge line until the horse is walking round you in ever-increasing circles. Stand at an angle from just behind his shoulder so that you are in a position to drive him forward. Assuming that he has been obedient to your previous training, he will already obey the command 'walk', so the whip must be used only as a guide to keep him out on the circle, and never to frighten or hit him.

When the horse is moving to your left, the rein will be in your left hand and the whip in your right; when he is going to the right, their positions will be reversed. Always work equally to left and right, and make sure that your commands are clear and that the horse obeys them.

Lungeing is quite a strain on a young horse, so do not work for more than about ten minutes at a time to begin with. You may harm young joints and tendons if you overdo it, and you will also make the horse bored and sour by sending him round in endless circles. If the horse plays up, as he is quite likely to do until he understands what you want, never get impatient: keep calm, and quietly insist on obedience. Lungeing, if done by a quiet, competent person, builds a sound foundation for the future, rather like teaching a child his ABC. By instilling discipline, you minimise the risk of accidents.

Intersperse the walking and trotting with frequent halts and changes of direction. Ensure that he stands still on the line of the circle and doesn't turn inwards or outwards. The horse should not be asked to canter until he is going freely forward at the walk and trot. Cantering in small circles puts a great strain on his legs, and should be kept to a minimum.

I wonder how often we stop to think just how much we ask of a horse during his initial training. With a horse that has been well handled since birth, the process is a gradual one and therefore not so alarming. Imagine, however, the feelings of a raw three-year-old who has not been handled previously, or perhaps a wild pony coming in off the moors. He is suddenly caught, confined for the first time in his life and made to accept strange objects in his mouth and on his back, has to live in unfamiliar surroundings, and is expected to understand and obey a jumble of human words that mean absolutely nothing to him. Is it any wonder that he gets confused, upset and sometimes distraught? We get impatient when the horse seems stupid and refuses to do as we ask, but we ought to put ourselves in his place – wouldn't we be confused too?

For this reason, never try to teach too much at a time. One lesson must be learnt thoroughly before you move on to the next. Unfortunately, when time means money, many horse trainers are forced to hurry the process, often with disastrous results. Racehorses, which are raced as two-year-olds, are broken when they are yearlings. This forcing of young minds and limbs is a controversial subject. However, as we are not dealing with racehorses, suffice it to say that the more time you allow your young horse to mature, both physically and mentally, the more thoroughly will he be able to learn the lessons you are teaching him.

Fitting the bit

Having got your horse going freely forward on the lunge, we now have to think of getting him used to having a bit in his mouth. Some horses are very nervous about having a bit inserted into their mouths for the first time. It is important that you do it gently and carefully – if you force it roughly into his mouth, you will find that your horse will become head-shy and difficult to bridle. The following method is an easy way of teaching a young horse to accept the bit without any fuss.

First, put on a headcollar. Remove the bit (an ordinary snaffle) from the bridle, and place the bridle over the ears in the normal way, but allowing the cheekpieces to hang loose on either side. Fasten the throat lash and noseband. Now, from the off side, attach the bit to the offside cheekpiece, and walk round to the near side. Very gently insert the bit into the mouth, using your thumb as already described on p. 28, and buckle it to the nearside cheekpiece. This method obviates the risk of upsetting a nervous horse by pinching or squeezing his ears as the bridle is put over his head.

The question of which type of bit to use on a young horse has caused controversy ever since man first sat on a horse's back. Everyone seems to have his own pet theory as to why one bit is more effective than another, and I think that one should keep an open mind on the subject. Unquestionably, what suits one horse will not necessarily suit another; each is an individual with his own particular way of going, conformation and temperament. It should be borne in mind, nevertheless, that the mouth of a young horse is soft and tender, and in order to keep it that way a mild bit is obviously preferable. The standard breaking bit has 'keys' attached which encourage the horse to play with it, thus inducing the flow of saliva and keeping the mouth moist. A dry mouth is more easily damaged by the action of the bit.

There is one fact, though, that is undeniable, and that is that a rider with 'good hands' will do no harm to the horse's mouth no matter which bit he is using, but one with rough, stiff hands will ruin it even though the horse is wearing the mildest of bits.

Fitting the roller or surcingle

Before putting a saddle on a young horse, he must be introduced to the roller or surcingle. The breaking roller is padded where it is placed on the horse's back, and has rings attached where side reins can be fastened if desired. The surcingle has no padding, and is often used to keep the saddle in position. The function of either, when used as a preliminary to the saddle, is to accustom the horse to having something tied around his middle.

Horses' reactions to this vary considerably. If the horse has been well handled from birth, he will probably take no notice, provided you do not fasten it too tightly at first. On the other hand, some horses that have had very little previous handling will object with such force that they can become a danger to both themselves and the trainer. I remember one horse I was breaking who threw himself against the loose-box door with such force that he knocked it clean off its hinges!

Ensure that the loose box is free of buckets or anything on which the horse could injure himself. Never tie him up; if he fights, he may become entangled in the rope. If you have just brought the horse in from the field, make sure that his back is clear of mud or grit.

Before actually fastening the buckle of the roller, prepare the horse carefully by letting it lie across his back. If he takes no notice of it, gradually tighten it up without fastening the buckle. If the horse tenses, he is not yet ready to have it done up properly. If you girth him up too tightly to start with, you will invite bucking and also teach him to 'blow himself out' (make himself rigid against the girth).

For your own safety, always ensure that you are standing between the horse and the door so that you can get out of the way quickly if the horse panics.

Saddling
When the horse accepts the roller quietly and without fuss you can progress to the saddle, which is put on in exactly the same way as described on pp. 23–6, making quite sure that it fits correctly.

Side reins
When the horse is going freely on the lunge, wearing a roller or a saddle, some people like to fit side reins. These are short reins which are attached to the bit and then fastened on each side to rings on the roller or, if the horse is wearing a saddle instead, to

the girth straps underneath the saddle flap. These reins are intended to teach the horse to yield to the bit, but care must be taken to ensure that they are not too tight; if they are, the horse will try to evade the bit by becoming 'overbent' – that is, tucking his nose into his chest – a bad fault which is difficult to cure.

Long reining

Long reining differs from lungeing in that the horse is worked not on a single lunge rein but between two reins, as shown below. The whole question of long reining seems to cause a great deal of controversy. Some trainers condemn it because they contend that, in the wrong hands, it could be injurious to the horse's mouth, and dangerous if the horse became entangled in the reins. This is true, but the argument only emphasises the fact that the training of a young horse should always be undertaken by an experienced person.

With safety in mind, long reining is an excellent method of preparing the horse for the unfamiliar experience of having a rider on his back. If done correctly and sympathetically, it not only instils discipline, but teaches the horse to obey the rein aids; gets him used to having pressure put on his sides, thus preparing him for the rider's leg aids; and also gets him accustomed to the reins touching his hindquarters and hind legs – a significant safety

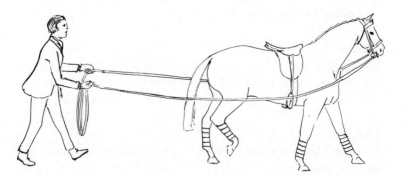

Long reining, showing the reins correctly adjusted through the tied stirrup irons

factor, as he is then not as likely to lash out in self-defence if someone touches him there unexpectedly. Another advantage of long reining is that it relieves the monotony of lungeing. A horse gets bored going round in endless circles; in the long reins he can be driven quietly along country lanes and through fields and farmyards, which is a wonderful education for a young horse as well as an additional method of exercising him without a rider on his back.

Another argument sometimes put forward against the use of long reins is that anything taught by this method can just as well be taught from the horse's back, and that doing so would save time. This cannot be denied, but time may be saved at the expense of safety. It is obvious that the more a horse is handled, and the wider his knowledge of the outside world – traffic, other animals, strange sights and sounds etc – *before* you get on his·back, the more relaxed and therefore the safer he will be when you start riding him.

There are some people who maintain that it is not possible to teach very much on the long reins anyway. They should visit the Spanish Riding School in Vienna, where the Lipizzaners are taught to perform some of the most advanced dressage movements on the long rein.

Only by learning from experienced people, and discussing their problems with various horses, will you be in a position to make up your own mind which of the diverse methods of breaking and schooling horses you prefer. To me, this variety of theories and ideas is one of the most interesting aspects of horse training. If you find that one method works better than another, then by all means try it; only by being open-minded and adaptable will you add to your store of knowledge and experience.

How to long rein
Put on the bridle that your horse has been wearing for lungeing, but minus the reins. Then you can use either the breaking roller or a saddle. If using a saddle, the stirrups must be let down and secured by a cord or strap, which is run underneath the horse on top of the girth; in this way the stirrups act as an

anchor through which the long reins are passed. You will need two lunge reins, or two long pieces of lightweight rope such as plough lines.

Initially, it is advisable to have an assistant to help you, as the horse may be nervous of the reins touching his flanks, and it would be safer to have someone to lead him at first.

Attach the reins to the bit, one on each side. Run them through the stirrups and back to your hands while you stand behind the horse – not too close – as though you were driving him in a plough. It is safer to do this in the box at first, until the horse becomes accustomed to the feel of the reins on his sides and flanks. When he is relaxed, and takes no notice of the reins being laid across the back of his hocks and across his quarters, you can take him outside. Go to the place where you have been lungeing him; here he will feel at home, and familiar with his surroundings.

Ask your assistant to lead him quietly round while you drive him, being very careful to handle his mouth with the utmost gentleness. As he gains confidence, the assistant should gradually walk further away from the horse, until his help can be dispensed with altogether.

Some trainers like to continue the circling process on the long reins, where they undoubtedly have more control over the horse's movements than on the lunge, but others prefer to drive him around the countryside, where they can accustom him to the sights and sounds of the outside world.

Backing the young horse

Hard and fast rules can seldom be laid down for the training of any horse, as each is an individual. Some are nervous and some lethargic; some learn very quickly, while others take a long time to assimilate anything. It is impossible to say how long the period of lungeing and long reining should last before the horse is asked to carry a rider. From the safety point of view, the more a horse is handled, and the less his preliminary training is hurried, the more likely you are to avoid an accident when you 'back' him (mount him for the first time). To boast of how quickly you can break in a horse is, in my view as foolish as boasting of how quickly you can drive from Land's End to London. In both cases, the faster you go the more risks you will run.

At the very minimum, a month of lungeing and long reining will be necessary before backing a youngster. The one drawback to taking too long is boredom. You will have to use your imagination to keep your horse interested. Never repeat the same thing for too long at a time. If you have an older, really quiet horse, it is an excellent idea to ride him out for short rides, leading the youngster alongside. This gets him used to walking beside another horse, and will pave the way for your first venture on the road when you back him.

After this careful preparation, the horse should be perfectly relaxed. He should be used to the stirrups hanging down by his sides during lungeing, and to the long reins touching him anywhere on his body.

The next step is to accustom him to having weight placed on his back. Initially this can be done in the confines of his box. Ask your assistant to hold him by the lead rein of his head-collar, while at the same time giving you a leg up so that you are leaning your weight across his back. On no account should you sit on him at this stage. Lean across his back from both sides so that he gets used to seeing your legs hanging down both his near and off sides. Let him walk forward a few steps, and wriggle about on his back until he totally ignores you. It is more comfortable for the horse if you do all this while he is wearing a saddle, which will help to protect his back. Raise and lower the saddle flaps a number of times so that he becomes accustomed to the noise and creak of saddlery.

Raise yourself up on your arms so that you are above the horse's eye level. It is often when the rider first sits upright that a horse becomes frightened, as he is not used to seeing anyone above him. Put the horse at his ease by talking to him and making a fuss of him. Only when the horse is completely relaxed with your weight on his back is he ready to be mounted properly.

There are many trainers who like to sit on a horse for the first time inside the stable, but I consider this to be risky : if he started to buck or rear, the rider could be thrown against the wall or could knock his legs against the sides of the box. Horses are unpredictable; however careful you are, there is no guarantee that a young horse will behave rationally. From the rider's point of view, it is safer to back the horse outside, where there is plenty of room. The exception, of course, is an indoor school, which is the ideal place, but few of us are lucky enough to have access to one.

If the horse is in familiar surroundings – where you have been lungeing him, for instance – he will not be nervous.

Never try to back a young horse on your own; an assistant must be at hand to lead him forward for the first steps. The best time to mount for the very first time is after the horse has been lunged and has settled down. Ask your assistant to lead him round for a few minutes while you lean across his back – an action with which he is already familiar. Now bring him to a halt, very carefully slide your right leg over, and sit gently in the saddle. If the preparation has been thorough, most horses will not mind at all, but the nervous type may tense up or try to buck. If this happens, it is essential that the rider stays put. Once the horse knows that he can dislodge the rider when he likes, he will undoubtedly try it on future occasions. For this reason, it is safer to put a neck strap on the horse so that you will have something to hang on to if he plays up.

Let him get used to your weight at the standstill before asking him to move forward. Be content with very little at first, and avoid giving him an excuse to buck. Allow the assistant to do all the work of asking him to walk forward. Do not use your legs at all until he is completely at ease, but hold the reins fairly short so that you can prevent him from getting his head down if he attempts to buck. Keep the first lesson very short. If you stay on his back for too long, he may become sour and bad-tempered. Remember that carrying a weight on his back goes against all his natural instincts, so be patient and don't ask for too much at a time.

Until you are confident that the horse is relaxed and happy, do not mount by putting your foot in the stirrup, but let the assistant give you a leg up for the first few lessons. There is a danger that you may accidentally poke your toe into the horse's side, causing him to jump away from you and trap your foot in the stirrup. Get him accustomed to having weight put on the stirrup by leaning on it with your hand at first.

As the horse gains confidence, you can begin to do more of the work yourself. Gradually start to use your leg and rein aids, and ask the assistant to allow the horse more freedom until eventually he is circling quietly at the end of the lungeing rein. Ride to both left and right, keeping the horse out on the perimeter of the circle. Don't be in too much of a hurry to trot – the unfamiliar movement of your body may well precipitate a buck if attempted too soon. When the horse is going freely, with no signs of tenseness, he can be taken off the lunge and ridden quietly on his own.

For the first week or so, it is advisable to lunge or long rein your horse each time before you mount; this will settle him down and take the edge off his high spirits. However quiet he seems, never take chances with him. Remember, he is still a baby with a baby's mind, and unable to use reason if suddenly frightened.

16

Riding for the Disabled

When you are fit and well your riding safety is your own responsibility, and you are able to decide for yourself whether to take risks or not, but spare a thought for those who are handicapped, either physically or mentally, and have to rely on others for their security. The Riding for the Disabled Association has not only spared a thought, but has worked tirelessly to form dedicated groups of helpers all over the country. Disabled children and adults are now encouraged to take an interest in horses and riding, which will not only widen their horizons and add to their interest in life, but will also improve their physical and mental health. They have an opportunity to forget their infirmities for a while in the companionship of a horse or pony and the stimulation of meeting and talking to people other than their close associates.

The idea of riding for the handicapped was suggested as early as the 1950s, but the Riding for the Disabled Association was actually registered in 1960. This chapter is not intended to give the history, nor to explain the organisation, of the RDA, but merely to give some idea of how the ordinary volunteer can help, and exactly what is entailed.

If you have never previously had any contact with mental or physical disability, you may be apprehensive and reluctant to take the first step in offering your services as a helper. This is understandable, but after that first step has been taken you will realise that your fears were completely unfounded. You will soon come to know the disabled riders so well that their handicaps will fade into the background, and it is their individual personalities that will become more important. It is not necessary to have any medical knowledge, nor even to know anything about horses. If you are 'horsey', of course, you will be a great asset, as the greater number of people there are who can deal knowledgeably with the horses and ponies, the safer the riders will be.

The following will give the volunteer some idea of what actually happens at a RDA meeting, though of course this procedure will not necessarily be followed exactly in every area. At every session there will be :

An instructor, who is responsible for teaching, and for seeing that the horses or ponies are suitable for each individual rider.
The helpers, who walk on either side of the rider to support those who need it, and to be there in case of emergencies for the benefit of those who are able to ride on their own. Some riders will only need one helper, while others may be able to manage with only a leader for the pony.
The leader, who leads the pony and is responsible for the pace at which he travels, his behaviour, and also for checking the tack.
The physiotherapist, who will have the medical knowledge to assist the helpers with any problems.
The ponies or horses, who are especially chosen for their manners and tractability in all circumstances. They are also individually suited in height and width to particular riders.

The duties of the helpers

When you arrive at the riding school or place where the riders have assembled, the ponies may already be tacked up and waiting. If not, and you are experienced with horses, you can help to tack them up. If you are at a riding school, you will soon learn the names of the ponies, and which saddles and bridles go on which animal.

If you know nothing about horses it doesn't matter – a friendly chat with the disabled riders will help you to get to know them. If you do not get much response at first from some of the more retarded ones, keep trying; they are bound to be shy with strangers.

A disabled rider with two helpers

The instructor will assign you to a particular rider, who may need a helper on each side of the pony, or only on one side, depending on the disability. Obviously the helper knowing most about horses will lead the horse or pony. Before the rider mounts, check that he is wearing a well-fitting hard hat with a chin strap, suitable shoes (see chapter 1) and comfortable jeans, jodhpurs or trousers. Gloves are important in cold weather. The leader should check the girth and ensure that the tack fits comfortably. Either the pony should be wearing a neck strap, or the saddle should be fitted with a leather handle: both are useful for the rider to hang on to, instead of pulling the pony's mouth, when trotting or jumping.

The lead rope must be attached either to the headcollar which is placed over the bridle, or to the cavesson noseband.

Mounting
A mounting block of some kind is essential. The leader must ensure that the pony stands perfectly still by standing in front and holding the reins on each side of the bit to prevent him from moving forward. The instructor or therapist will assist with any difficult cases that need special care in lifting or that may require certain equipment such as belts or harnesses.

One helper should stand on the off side of the pony to guide the rider's foot into the stirrup. Do not be in too much of a hurry. Allow the rider time to do as much for himself as he is able : it will encourage him, and the physical exertion will do him good. When he is safely mounted, the instructor will check the leathers to ensure that they are the right length for that particular rider. (There is no general rule here, as the rider's disability will dictate the correct length for him.)

When you are satisfied that the\ rider is comfortable, move off and walk quietly round until the other riders are mounted. If there is only one helper, he should walk on the opposite side to the leader of the pony. This not only ensures that there is someone on both sides in an emergency, but gives both leader and helper more room to walk.

The leader

As leader, you must always be alert and ready to anticipate trouble before it happens. For example, if the pony lays back his ears or tenses up, there is a reason for it, and you must find out what it is at once. The pony behind may be getting too close, or the animal may have seen some object that is frightening him. Warn the helper to stay close, and put a steadying hand on the rider if necessary. Always ensure that there is at least a horse's length between you and the animal in front. Never make sharp turns that may upset the rider's balance; and, if on grass, be prepared for the pony trying to eat, and don't let him get his head down.

When riding on the road, keep to the left and lead the pony from his off side so that you place yourself between him and the traffic. The helper, of course, if there is only one, remains on the near side. Encourage the rider to say thank you to considerate motorists, and teach him some simple signals such as raising the arm to turn right or left.

Concentrate on the job in hand – if you start chatting to other helpers you may forget the rider, and this is when accidents happen. If belts or harness are used on the rider, don't use them to lean on; they are there for the rider's safety, not to drag you along.

Allow the rider himself to steer within the bounds of safety. The role of the leader is rather like that of a co-pilot; he allows the rider to take control according to his capabilities, but takes over immediately a crisis occurs. Remember, though, that the instructor is there to do the teaching. You can help the rider by explaining quietly any instruction he has not understood, but if you keep nagging at him to do this and that he will only become bored.

Try to make riding fun by being relaxed and good-humoured; some of the severely sub-normal may not make any progress at all, but the enjoyment they get from just being on a horse and meeting other people in different surroundings will have a beneficial effect both physically and mentally. If a beginner is stiff and scared, you can do much by your own confident and happy manner to help him to relax. A smile and a joke will do a great deal more good than a dictatorial attitude. If you find that your rider is getting over-tired or uncomfortable inform the instructor.

To sum up, the motto of the competent helper could well be, 'Be Awake! Be Aware!'

You may on occasions feel discouraged by the apparent lack of progress of some of the riders, but don't give up; your patience and understanding are probably contributing more than you will ever be able to appreciate.

Appendix:

SOME USEFUL ADDRESSES

Association of British Riding
    Schools,
Chesham House,
56 Green End Road,
Sawtry,
Huntingdon,
Cambridgeshire

British Field Sports Society,
59 Kennington Road,
London, S.E.1

British Horse Society,
National Equestrian Centre,
Kenilworth,
Warwickshire

British Pony Society,
Smale Farm,
Wisborough Green,
Billingshurst,
Sussex

British Show Hack and Cob
    Association,
National Equestrian Centre,
Kenilworth,
Warwickshire

British Veterinary Association,
7 Mansfield Street,
London, W.1

Hunters' Improvement and
    National Light Horse
    Breeding Society,
8 Market Square,
Westerham,
Kent

National Foaling Bank,
The Meretown Stud,
Newport,
Salop

Riding for the Disabled
    Association,
Avenue R,
National Agricultural Centre,
Kenilworth,
Warwickshire

Royal Society for the Prevention
    of Cruelty to Animals,
Causeway,
Horsham,
Sussex

How many mistakes can you spot?

How many mistakes can you spot?

Top left Rider allowing horse to get too close to heels of another; man smoking near hay shed; fence made of barbed wire; discarded horse shoes, broken bottle, and pitchfork left lying around; bucket left where it can be knocked over.

Bottom left Single rein curb on bridle of ridden horse too severe; saddle slipping on led pony – girth not fastened correctly; saddle left where horses could tread on it; stirrups not run up.

Top right Window opposite door of loose box causing through draught; mucking-out tools left where horses could knock them over; saddles thrown down carelessly; wheelbarrow left in middle of yard; horse with rug on allowed to run around loose; same horse has no pad underneath surcingle to protect spine; rider dismounting incorrectly and has dropped reins; haynet tied too low – horse gets foot through it; horse tied with bridle instead of headcollar; no quick release knots; stirrups not run up.

Bottom right Female rider not wearing hat, has bare legs, and is wearing plimsolls, necklace and dangling earrings; same rider is holding reins incorrectly, and pulling bit out of horse's mouth; male rider mounting from incorrect position, with wrong leg in stirrup and not holding the reins; grooming utensils left lying around.

Index